CONTENTS

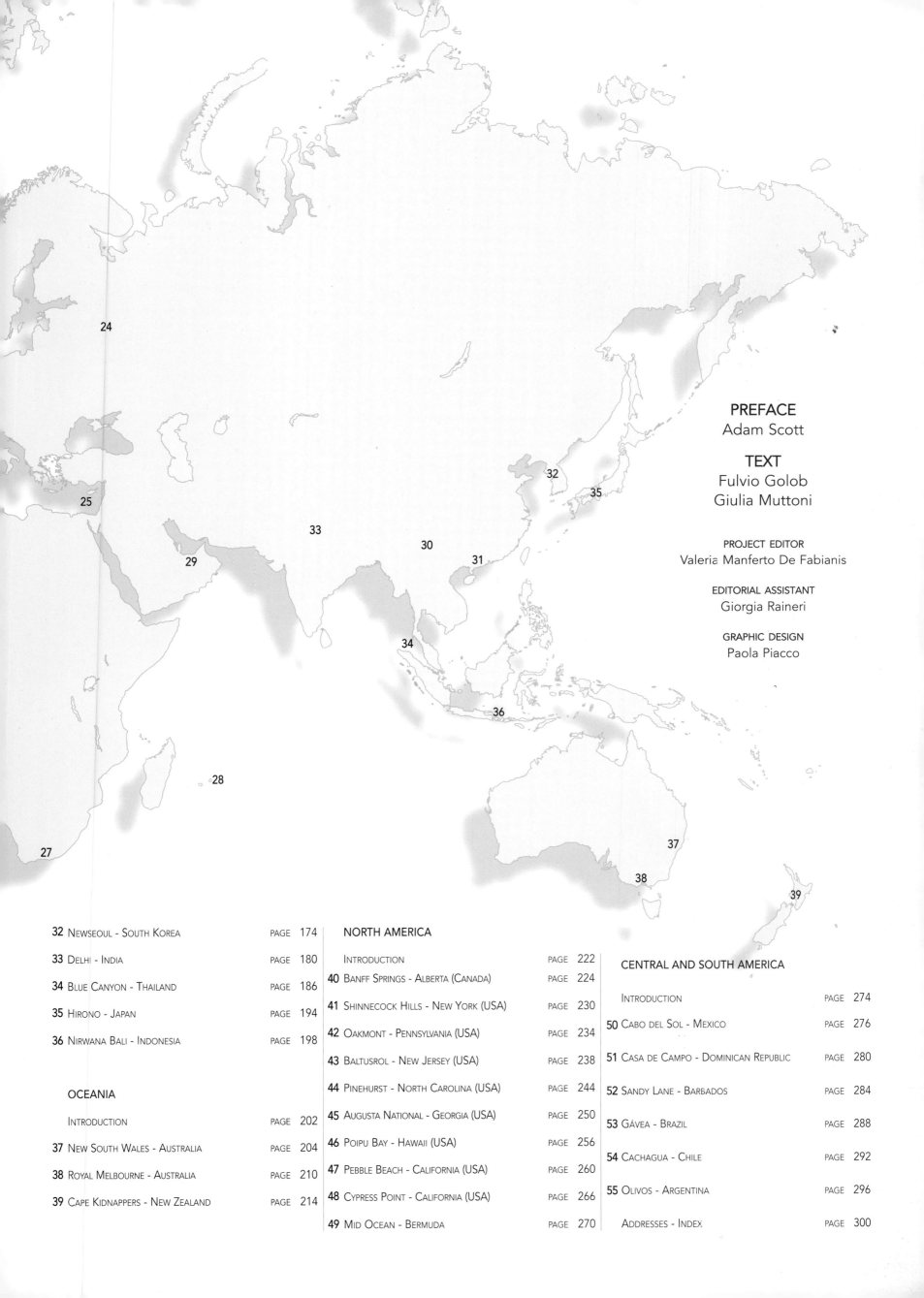

PREFACE
Adam Scott

TEXT
Fulvio Golob
Giulia Muttoni

PROJECT EDITOR
Valeria Manferto De Fabianis

EDITORIAL ASSISTANT
Giorgia Raineri

GRAPHIC DESIGN
Paola Piacco

PREFACE

One of the enduring aspects of golf, and indeed perhaps a major reason for its timeless popularity, is that its courses exhibit the natural characteristics of the region or even the country being played in. A course becomes not only a venue for a sporting contest, but a snapshot highlighting the best features of an area. From its humble beginnings on the windswept links of Scotland, the game of golf has spread to all the continents of the world and is enjoyed by millions of people. Every minute of every day, no matter the weather, the economic conditions, or other vagaries of life, tee pegs are being put in the ground on first tees, with the participants gleeful in the knowledge that for the next few hours at least they can forget everything else and just indulge their passion for arguably the greatest game of all. To my mind, and in my experience, no other game can provide so much varied experience in a relatively short period of time. It is not just the challenge of negotiating the obstacles designed by the course architects, of trying to perfect the complex swing, or reading the break on a four-foot putt, but also the enjoyment of being with friends, or making new ones, being outdoors and simply walking around acres of beautiful countryside. When I was learning to play the game it was explained to me that playing a round of golf was "a round in life." Dealing with the challenges, often unfair, that a course can bring, understanding the psyche of ones playing partner or opponent, or simply enjoying the moment for what it is all parallel what we have to face off the golf course in our day-to-day lives. Through the development of the game of golf came the handicapping system, allowing players of all abilities to compete against each other as equals. This unique aspect has created the wonderful spirit in the game that continues today, the opportunity for the most accomplished player to be upstaged by someone of lesser skill who nevertheless plays the same golf course, under the same conditions. This has allowed the participants of the game, whatever their culture, to embrace golf and make the game their own.

This book showcases a diverse collection of golf courses. Many will be famous and known to most golfers. Many may have been seen on television hosting professional tournaments and some may be no more than a name read on the page of a magazine. What is certain is that every course featured here offers its own individual characteristics, represents its geographical area, and is an important ingredient in the recipe that is world golf. It may also serve as an opportunity for golfers to visualize and appreciate courses that they have never visited, perhaps encouraging some debate with golfing partners as to the attributes of one course or another. We can, and should, celebrate the never-ending variations that the recipe for golf courses allows. There is no one recipe, no law as to what the ingredients should be. Instead we should savor every finished product, every flavor we are offered, and appreciate the differences. The spirit of the game is the same, from the manicured landscapes of Augusta National Golf Club to the sandscape courses in the outback of Australia.

Traveling the world to play golf, as I do, is a blessing that I never take for granted. To have visited countries, cities, and villages that I would likely have not otherwise known is a great fortune. In every instance the playing field has been different, the setting unique and the people a part of the worldwide golf culture. Never has there been one day the same as another. Never has a day not produced some drama or joy. Every day has indeed been "a walk in life." I hope this book encourages you to walk with me.

Adam Scott

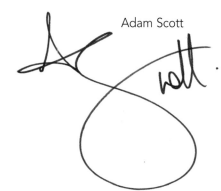

INTRODUCTION

Golf is a special sport. It is probably the oldest sport and definitely the one that is played in the most varied and extreme conditions. It is also a sport that has left its mark on the moon and in space. The story of golf begins many centuries ago, with a distant relative played in Roman times called *paganica*. Unfortunately, little is known about its rules today, but we do know that it required a bent club and a leather ball stuffed with wool or feathers. From those distant times we move swiftly to February 1971, when on the surface of the moon Alan Shepard tried hitting a golf ball with his Wilson number 6. His cumbersome spacesuit and thick gloves forced him to try and hit it with one hand, but after a first poor shot he struck the ball a great distance thanks to the absence of air and reduced gravity. After the moon, in November 2006 it was in space itself that the Russian astronaut Mikhail Tyurin, from the international station orbiting around the earth, shot a ball into orbit using a gold-plated club.

Back on earth, golf is played in a myriad of extraordinary environments. Starting in the far north, at Ulukhahtok, in the Northwestern Territories of Canada, at over 70 degrees latitude, all the way south to the other side of the world in Tierra del Fuego, on the southern tip of South America, where there is the Ushuaia Golf Club, almost on the treacherous and fearsome Cape Horn. In between these two clubs there are a further 31,000 to 32,000 courses, half of which are concentrated in the United States. In terms of altitude, golf has no rivals. For example, it is played at 214 ft (65 m) below sea level at the Furnace Creek Golf Club in Death Valley, California, and at 10,800 ft (3300 m) at the La Paz Golf Club, Bolivia.

To the early pioneers of the game this modern, world-embracing phenomenon would seem incredible. It began as a pastime in Scotland and has developed in a way that was almost unthinkable even a few decades ago. One of the main reasons for this is the beauty of the game, which is riveting and capable of charming even the most skeptical. No other sport requires such a keen application to the game to reach even an average level of skill, and no other sport has the possibility of modifying its playing strategy in almost infinite ways, based on mathematical schemes as well as requiring imagination. From official matches to a friendly game, from the classic point system to the Stableford system, from a single to a double or team match, from foursomes to greensomes, from pro-am to matchplay – there really is an amazing variety. But golf's real winning factor is where it is played, often at gorgeous locations and always surrounded by nature. Perfect places to combine a sporting occasion with a social one, with the possibility of turning a chance meeting on a fairway into an opportunity to make friends or to conduct business.

The financial and economic aspects of golf are extremely important. It is almost always the case that anything built beside a golf course increases in value. Golf resorts are hugely successful tourist destinations and golf-related tourism is now a global industry worth tens of billions of dollars. The manufacture of the great range of golf products, particularly equipment, is also a so lucrative business. For instance, approximately over one billion golf balls are produced each year. To give an example of the economic importance of the game, let us look at the latest data available in the annual *Golf Economy Report*. The total turnover of golf-related businesses almost reaches an astronomical 76 billion dollars, which would rise to 195 billion f employment was taken into consideration. This is a mighty industry that in the U.S. alone provides work for more than two million people, supplying the needs of 30 million golfers, with a turnover higher than sectors such as newspapers or cinema.

Throughout the different continents we discover different attitudes and approaches towards golf, which promote new traditions, ways of playing, course design, and so forth but all still based on the same basic principles. The original foundation of the game is unquestionably Scottish, where the first clubs were founded and where the game was established and its rules first codified. It was then taken into continental Europe and the United States, which has resulted in the great his-

2-3 Cape Kidnappers, New Zealand: golf and nature form a true spectacle.

4-5 Carnoustie, Scotland: the most beautiful and most challenging links in the world.

toric rivalry between these two continents of golfers. A rivalry that has found its ultimate expression in the fascinating and fiercely contested Ryder Cup. This biennial competition was established in 1927 and was sponsored by a Samuel Ryder, a British entrepreneur who sold garden seeds and who commissioned the famous golden trophy. Initially, it was the best British players against the best players from the U.S.A., played alternately in Europe and America. However, the U.S. won so often that it was decided to include the best European players, which brought in players from Denmark, France, Germany, Italy, Spain, and Sweden. Since 1990, in the years between Ryder Cups, there has also been a female version, the Solheim Cup.

Of course the most important tournaments in the men's game are the four Grand Slams, also known as the Major Championships, which, in order of when they are played, are the Masters, the U.S. Open, the Open Championship, and the PGA Championship. The oldest of all is the Open Championship, often called the British Open outside of Britain, which was first held on 17th October 1860 at the Prestwick Golf Club course, about 30 miles (50 km) from Glasgow. Today, there are nine courses used in rotation to host the most prestigious championship in the world: St. Andrews, Carnoustie, Muirfield, Turnberry, and the five "Royals" – Troon, St. George's, Birkdale, Lytham & St. Annes, Liverpool (seven of these courses are included in this book). Of the other three Majors, which are all held in the U.S., the Masters distinguishes itself for being the only one with a fixed venue at the marvelous and inaccessible garden that, outside of the competition week, is the Augusta National, Georgia. Designed by the great Bobby Jones in 1934, it became more famous than the U.S. Open itself, which started in 1895 and still involves the country's most beautiful and most difficult courses. Of these we have selected a few to describe in this book, including Pinehurst, Oakmont, Pebble Beach, Baltusrol, and Shinnecock Hills. The same goes for the fourth Major, PGA Championship established in 1916 and considered less prestigious than the others, even though it attracts first-class players and it is played on high-class courses.

If in Britain, Ireland, and the U.S.A. golf has been an established and popular sport for some time, in continental Europe it often had a hard time establishing itself. However, in the last few decades great progress has been made and the number of golfers has grown significantly throughout the continent. For example, in Sweden, the country with the most golfers outside Britain despite having only a few months a year available to play, and Spain, where they have constructed some amazing golf resorts and courses in several regions. The Costa del Sol is probably the best-known golf destination in Spain, so much so that it is known as the "Costa del Golf," and in the area around Malaga alone there are 55 clubs. Amongst these is the magnificent Valderrama, which in 1997 established Spain as a true golfing nation by hosting an unforgettable Ryder Cup.

In Africa and South America golf is still not a hugely popular sport and is confined to a few, restricted areas. Oceania can rely on two countries that boast excellent golf traditions. In Australia as much as in New Zealand the game is considered a national sport, and there are numerous golfers and exceptional courses, which definitely deserve to be visited. However, the exciting new frontier in golf is Asia, which, from the United Arab Emirates all the way to Japan, is rapidly discovering a deep passion for holes, clubs, balls, and the whole industry of golf. Millions and millions of players fly from one end of the continent to the other to pursue their favorite sport. There are spectacular courses being constructed in Asia, particularly in Thailand, Indonesia, Korea, and, recently, China. Golf only returned to the country with biggest population in the world about 25 years ago, and only in the last decade has its popularity exploded with the planning and creation of hundreds of resorts and courses. The greatest example is the enormous Mission Hills, which is in the *Guinness Book of Records* with its 12 courses.

With the arrival of China on the world golf stage, West and East now share a common passion. The game of golf has become truly global and in this book we can take a fascinating journey around the world, continent by continent, from one amazing course to another.

12-13 Cypress Point, California: the trio of the 15th, 16th, and 17th holes, recognized as one of the best sequences in the world.

14-15 The tough bunkers next to the 11th green at Spyglass Hills, one of the four superlative 18 holes of the Pebble Beach Resort, California.

EUROPE

Netherlands or Scotland? Medieval history more or less points to the Dutch as the originators of golf. The word golf deriving from kolf or kolve, meaning "stick" in the female form in the Flemish dialect. It was mentioned as early as 1300, when the inhabitants of the town of Loenen enjoyed hitting a ball with a wooden tool. However, golf certainly owes its actual birth to the passion of the Scottish. Supposedly, the oldest golf layout is the Old Links in Musselburgh, a few miles from Edinburgh, which boasts an uninterrupted history of golf since 1672, even though Mary I of Scotland probably played in this area as early as 1567. Soon after Musselburgh come the Prestwick and the Old Course in St Andrews, which today is one of the world's most famous clubs. Walking St. Andrews' legendary fairways, facing its large bunkers and double greens is almost every golfer's dream. Playing here, seeing the majestic clubhouse nearby, so rich with history, can disarm the greatest of champions. Even the most experienced pros will feel their legs shake a little when on the 1st tee the starter calls out their names to prepare for the first drive. From Edinburgh and its surroundings, golf spread quickly throughout all the British Isles in the second half of the 19th century. Britain has abundant grass and rain, plenty of coastal areas with few trees where links could be created on sandy soils that were not fertile enough for agriculture.

Golf was then introduced to the continental Europe, exported by British noblemen, many of whom were enthusiastic sportsmen, passionately inventing or perfecting all kinds of sports, such as tennis, rugby, cricket, and snooker. Today, golf is played everywhere in Europe and though Great Britain and Ireland are still the biggest golfing nations, Germany, France, Holland, Sweden, and Spain also have significant and growing numbers of courses and players.

According to the EGA (European Golf Association), Europe has had more than four million golfers for some time now, even though the data actually refers to those who are members of various national federations. The most interesting areas for the future development of the game are west-central Europe and parts of the Mediterranean region, where golf has taken longer to grow in popularity. There are now almost 7000 courses in Europe, from the great classic courses and historic clubs of Great Britain and Ireland, which have shaped the very nature of golf, to the many magnificent courses in continental Europe. We chose 25 of the most beautiful courses to include in this truly distinguished golf anthology.

16 left The rigor of the Carnoustie Championship Course.

16 center The legendary Old Course of St. Andrews.

16 right In the far north at Royal Dornoch.

17 Loch Lomond: Scotland's most beautiful parkland.

18-19 An aerial view of the Halmstad Golfklubb, located in Tylösand on a promontory of the Kattegat strait, which separates Sweden from Denmark. Though the air is salty and the sea bellows, it cannot be seen from any of the holes.

18 bottom From the historic clubhouse, designed in 1938 by Hakon Ahlberg, there are some interesting views of the holes. Majestically situated, it offers many services: as well as bars and restaurants, there is also a large pool with water jets.

19 The 13th hole is a par 4 of 395 yards (361 m) with ample fairways that narrow down near the two bunkers on the right. The North Course hosted the 2007 Solheim Cup.

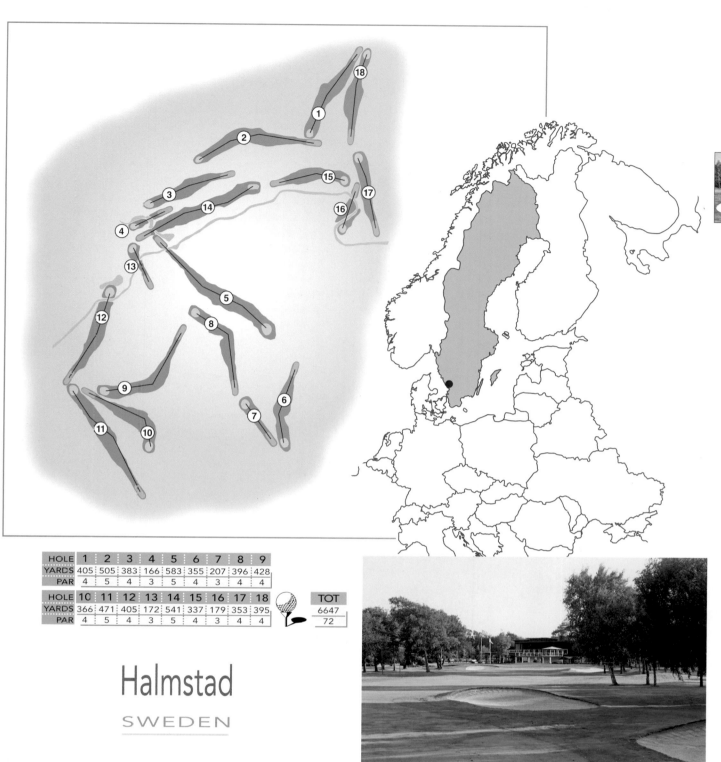

HOLE	1	2	3	4	5	6	7	8	9
YARDS	405	505	383	166	583	355	207	396	428
PAR	4	5	4	3	5	4	3	4	4

HOLE	10	11	12	13	14	15	16	17	18		TOT
YARDS	366	471	405	172	541	337	179	353	395		6647
PAR	4	5	4	3	5	4	3	4	4		72

Halmstad

SWEDEN

It may seem strange, but Sweden is one of the most golf-crazy countries in the world: with 480 courses and 580,000 players from a population of about 9 million, which means that about 6.5 percent of Swedes plays golf.

The first course, Gothenburg, was created in 1902, followed two years later by Stockholm and thereafter new courses appeared steadily. Although Europe's golf boom in the 1980s also affected Sweden, it was in the following decade that the country's number of courses increased by a whopping 72 percent, thanks to the great amount of available land and the increasing popularity of the sport. This popularity was due to tour victories by professionals such as Jesper Parnevik, Carl Pettersen, Per Ulrik Johansson, and female pros such as Catrin Nilsmark, Carin Koch, and especially Annika Sorenstam – a legendary female golf hero for years.

The problem in this country – 930 miles (1500 km) in length from the same latitude as the Danish capital to beyond the Arctic Circle – is that there are very few months in which it is possible to play. Typically, there are five or six months available, though fewer in the north and more in the southern region of Skaane, near Malmö. It is also true that during the summer months the days are so long that you can play 36 consecutive holes, while in the northern region you can tee off at midnight. Another alternative is to play in the snow, which is why the north-central areas have increasing numbers of courses that are open year-round and where it is possible to play on white fairways and greens.

Among the green greens, is the Halmstad in Tylösand, situated on a promontory in the Kattegat strait, which separates Sweden from Denmark. Here you can breathe the salty air and hear the booming of the sea, although it is not visible from any of the holes. The history of the club is rather eventful. It was founded in 1930 and during the first years a temporary course was used in a military training center, while construction of the 18 holes in Tylösand, designed by Rafael Sundblom, was begun in 1935. In 1963 a permit was granted to build another nine holes, designed by Nils Sköl, and these are the holes that, along with the following nine of the original course, make up the present-day North Course.

20-21 An historic moment: the legendary female golfer Annika Sorenstam and the European team during the 2007 Solheim Cup on the 16th tee, one of the most famous holes in all of Sweden. It is a par 3 with a raised tee and a long and narrow green.

20 bottom During the competition, Paula Creamer from the U.S., like many other players, shot into the bunker protecting the left side of the green on the 6th hole.

21 Natalie Gulbis, another American pro, studies her putt on the 5th hole, the longest par 5 of the course (583 yards/533 m). The green is flush with bunkers on both sides.

Finally, in 1975 the work on another nine holes (created by Frank Pennink) began, which together with the first nine of the old course gave birth to the South Course. Over the years, constant updating was carried out both by Pennink and his successor Donald Steel, so that one of Sweden's oldest clubs is also one of the most modern ones, as well as one of the few to have 36 holes.

Of the two courses, the North is the most famous. It hosted the Solheim Cup in 2007, the female version of the Ryder Cup. It is a course of great character that unfolds amongst sandy dunes in the forest, meandering fairways that do not skimp on bunkers, a creek and natural crags, a natural fast plateau or elongated greens, and bizarre doglegs, all embellished by a perfectly manicured turf that is challenging in freezing winters and short summers.

Halmstad

One of the first things that astonishes is the space, which is so ample that each hole feels as though it is alone on the course. The long rows of trees lining the fairways do not only efficiently shield players from what happens on the other courses, but they also make up for the lack of rough. It might not be impossible to find the ball if it disappeared among the tree trunks, but the hard thing is finding the path to return to the fairway. Beware of the wind coming from the west, which chills your very bones. The 16th hole is one of the most famous in Sweden, where the fate of many a tournament has been decided. It is a par 3, 179 yards (164 m), with the wind typically blowing from the left. From the raised tee, players must reach the long and narrow green protected in the front and on the right by a creek.

Halmstad

22 top Test shots from the bunker: Nicole Castrale practices before facing the European team.

22 center At the tee shot on the 16th, players must clear a creek in front and right of the green. Normally it is played with the wind from the left. This hole has decided the outcome of many tournaments.

22 bottom Considered to be one of the most beautiful holes in Sweden, the 12th is a par 4 of 405 yards (370 m). It is best to aim straight for the right side of the fairway and hope to find a flat lie.

22-23 The 9th hole is a long par 4 of 428 yards (391 m) with a right

dogleg. The Halmstad Club was initially built in 1930, but construction in Tylösand began five years later under the architect Rafael Sundblom. In 1963 another nine holes, designed by Nils Sköl, were added and they complemented the second nine of the first course, and so the North Course was born.

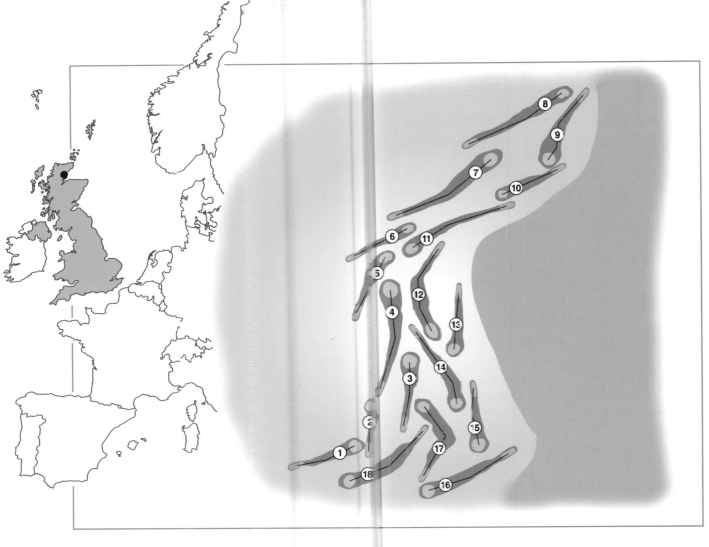

Royal Dornoch

UNITED KINGDOM

HOLE	1	2	3	4	5	6	7	8	9
YARDS	331	177	414	427	354	163	463	396	496
PAR	4	3	4	4	4	3	4	4	5

HOLE	10	11	12	13	14	15	16	17	18
YARDS	147	446	507	166	445	319	402	405	456
PAR	3	4	5	3	4	4	4	4	4

TOT
6514
70

In 1727, in Dornoch – a town full of history, where the first human settlements date back 4000 years – Janet Horne, the last Scottish "witch" was burned at the stake. In 1616, more than a century before, golf was already being played on the coastal dunes near the town, as recorded in ancient documents stating that the local authorities considered this sport as a waste of precious time that could be otherwise used for more profitable activities. Local approval or not, this makes Dornoch one of the oldest golf course in the world. However the Dornoch Golf Club was not founded until 1877 and it was only in 1886 that first nine natural holes were turned into a true course by Old Tom Morris, who three years later doubled them.

At the beginning of the 20th century golf was revolutionized by the invention of the modern golf ball with rubber thread wound up around a central core, which replaced the ones made of gutta-percha. The use of a faster ball forced John Sutherland, secretary of the club for over 50 years, to have the course redesigned. For a while Dornoch was the fifth longest British course and in 1906 it received the coveted 'Royal' title from King Edward VII. In the same period a second course was established, the Ladies, where all the town children could play for free. During the Second World War, four holes of the championship course and all 18 of the Ladies were confiscated in order to use them as a minor military airport. At the end of the war the compensation given by the Ministry of Aviation allowed the reconstruction of the championship course. This meant widening the holes towards Embo, as well as re-creating nine holes of what was then renamed the Struie Course, which only many years later returned to the status of 18 holes.

In the 21st century, Royal Dornoch continues to have a timeless charm and golf purists make a pilgrimage to it at least once. A true pilgrimage it is too, as the five hours from Glasgow, 600 miles (965 km) from London and 50 miles (79 km) from Inverness (the northernmost British city) mean that it does not make most golf itineraries.

24 As early as 1616 people played golf on the coastal dunes of Dornoch. The Dornoch Golf Club was founded in 1877 and only in 1886 were the initial nine natural holes transformed into a course by Tom Morris.

24-25 It has an ancient feel, but it is modern and functional. The clubhouse welcomes players on the green of the 18th. Even from the Royal Golf Hotel, next to the 1st tee, there is a fine view of the course.

*25 bottom Dornoch is relatively
remote, which is one reason why
it has never hosted international
tournaments. But golf purists
always make at least one trip to
this wild Scottish jewel during
their lives.*

Royal Dornoch

26-27 *The bunker, generally round and steep-walled, the depressions, and the knolls and mounds, punish less-than-perfect shots: it is difficult to attack the greens.*

26 bottom *A par 4 of 405 yards (370 m), the 17th hole is flanked on both sides by thick gorse bushes. A diagonal 38 yard (35 m) drop cuts the fairway 180 yards (165 m) from the starting position.*

27 top A plateau green for the 6th hole, a par 3 with thick gorse bushes on the left hillside, three bunkers on the left edge of the green, and a wide on the right.

27 bottom Once in a while, the Royal Dornoch gives a player a breather, with a flat green. The space seems to stretch out, aided by the ample view of the sea.

It is this very isolation that excludes it from the rotation of the Open Championship.

Wild and wonderful when the gorse explodes in early summer, speckling the green fairways and the white beaches with a shining yellow, Royal Dornoch offers all that a golfer can ask from a perfect tour: a beautiful environment, a very serious but honest test and fast yet delicate greens, with their tone-rich contours. The raised greens, many of which are built on natural plateaus that make for a difficult approach, are the trademark of Dornoch's most famous son, Donald Ross (1872–1948). He was a famed pro and greenkeeper here, before moving to America and becoming one of the most famous golf architects. These greens are a trademark that can be found in his other, later creations, first and foremost the Pinehurst N.2.

Not too long according to modern standards, 6513 yards (5956 m), with a simple layout (out and in), the Championship Course demands great accuracy in order to avoid the bunkers, dunes, bumps, and hills that penalize ill-fated shots. But the true hazard is the wind, which can blow on different days from various directions, making it seem a radically different course and causing the choice of clubs to be very problematic. Perhaps this is also why Tom Watson, who in 1981 came here to play a round, ended up playing three, stating: "it's the most fun I've ever had on a golf course." Of all the many unforgettable holes, the 6th, known as Whinny Brae, deserves a mention. It is a par 3 of 163 yards (149 m) that separates the holes on the floor from the ones that are raised. There are thick bushes on the left hill and three bunkers on the left edge of the plateau green, which is protected at the entrance by a large bunker. There is a 12 ft (3,5 m) fall the rear and right of the green.

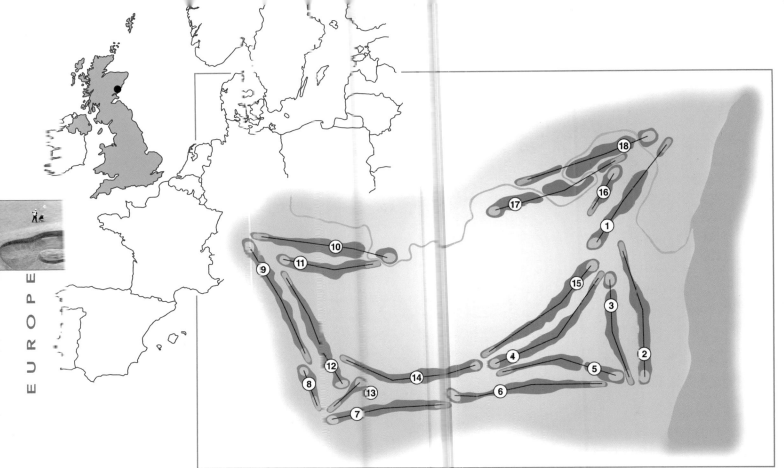

Carnoustie

UNITED KINGDOM

HOLE	1	2	3	4	5	6	7	8	9
YARDS	401	435	337	375	387	520	394	167	413
PAR	4	4	4	4	4	5	4	3	4

HOLE	10	11	12	13	14	15	16	17	18		TOT
YARDS	446	352	479	151	483	459	245	433	444		6941
PAR	4	4	5	3	5	4	3	4	4		72

Beautiful and difficult, this is the Carnoustie Championship Course. Actually, it is really difficult. So much so that the Americans nicknamed it "Car-nasty" for its ability to challenge even the best golfers. The Frenchman Jean Van de Velde and the Spaniard Sergio García know something about this in 1999 and in 2007 they literally threw the possibility of winning the Open Championship to the wind on the super-tricky 18th hole. And the 2007 winner himself, Padraig Harrington, risked ruining everything when, during the last round, he ended up in the water twice also on the 18th. For these and many other similar episodes, the Championship is considered the most difficult course among the ones included in the British Open rotation.

Carnoustie is on the east coast of Scotland, slightly north of St. Andrews and not far from Dundee. Golf here has ancient roots. In fact it seems that, as certified by documents of the day, it was played as early as 1527, a quarter of a century before St. Andrews. The original course only had ten holes and often interweaved with the Barry Burn, the small and lethal stream that still winds its way across the 17th (Island) and 18th (Home). It was the construction of the coastal railroad in 1838 that brought in groups of new players from Edinburgh, anxious to try the famous links. And some 30 years later the growing popularity of the course brought about its restructuring. It was 1867 and the legendary Old Tom Morris was in charge of the work. He expanded the course to 18 holes. But only at the end of the century, in 1890, did the land on which the Championship Course stood become the property of the inhabitants of Carnoustie. The Count of Dalhousie decided to sell it to the community, making it "available forever for its fun." Today, near this famous course there are the Burnside Course and the Budden Links, property of Carnoustie and managed by the Angus council, one of the 32 counties in which Scotland is divided into.

The great hotel that rises next to the tee of the 1st hole (Cup) and the green of the 18th offers players every comfort. The clubhouse, on the other hand, located on the other side of the road that flanks the golf courses, is a comfy building though lacking basic facilities. This is where the Carnoustie Golf Club, founded in 1842, has its headquarters. Its symbol consists of a leafy tree with three crows flying above (according to tradition, the name Carnoustie derives from the ancient name "Craw's Nestie," or crow's nest).

The Championship has a double "C" structure and, like the Old Course at St. Andrews, it does not come back to the clubhouse halfway through.

28 Pictured from above, the 18th holes of the Championship Course in Carnoustie make a double C shape. Like many old Scottish courses, it does not return to the clubhouse at the end of the front nine.

28-29 The meandering flow of the Barry Burn, the insidious water hazard that runs through the 17th and 18th holes of the Carnoustie Championship Course. In the background, the hotel serves as a clubhouse for this Scottish course.

29 bottom The green of the 10th South America, the only hole with a tall-trunk tree as part of the game.

30 top One of the large bunkers protecting the green on the 13th Whins, a tough par 3 of 161 yards (147 m).

30 bottom The 9th hole of the Carnoustie Championship

Course is a nice par 4 of 413 yards (378 m), with a thick group of trees on the left side acting as the out of bounds. The large gorse bushes are a delicate natural hazard along the entire hole.

For this reason, there is a small bar located behind the green of the beautiful 10th hole (South America), guarded by an embracing curve of the Barry Burn and by a large plant, the only tall tree that affects the game on the course. Also known as the "The Beast" in reference to its difficulty, the Carnoustie Championship is one extraordinary links. The course is full of enormous gorse bushes, which have beautiful yellow flowers in spring, but for the rest of the year grow long spiky thorns – the best deterrent for whoever wanders off looking for a ball in its tangled branches. The Championship is especially famous for the aforementioned Barry Burn, which sinuously cuts it in several points, and for its treacherous bunkers. Some are enormous, such as the twin "Spectacles" which give the 14th hole the hardest one, its name. Others are small, hidden, and capable of stealing more than a

shot from the unlucky golfer who ends up playing it. We cannot forget the wind, of course, which on the North Sea coast is always a formidable opponent, as well as the wavy fast greens.

Of all the most beautiful holes, besides those already mentioned, the 6th (Hogan's Alley) deserves a mention. It is a par 5 dedicated to the American champ who, in 1953, played his only Open in Great Britain at Carnoustie. Naturally he won, thanks in large part to the extraordinary way he played this hole. The most important golf competition in the world was held at the Championship for the first time in 1931, after a course review by James Braid in 1926. Later on it hosted another six Opens: 1937, 1953, 1968, 1975, 1999, and 2007. Before the 1937 Open, James Wright redesigned the last three holes, making them into one of the most infamous finales of all the world's great golf courses.

Carnoustie

30-31 The North Sea caresses Carnoustie's Championship Course, but never comes into play. The lack of hills emphasizes the wind's role, which on this course can become the main protagonist.

31 bottom The bunkers in Carnoustie are tough, tricky, and above all well-positioned along the course. To avoid them it is essential to adopt a careful game strategy and a make a wise choice of clubs.

32-33 Carnoustie is a very challenging links which requires a high level of skill. The Championship Course belongs to the group of nine courses that, in turn, have the honor of hosting the Open Championship, the world's most famous competition.

32 bottom The Championship Course at Carnoustie is one of the best examples of a traditional British links, with no trees on the course. The challenges are the pot bunkers, the tall rough next to the holes, and in the wind, which is often fairly strong.

33 top The famous Barry Burn (the water hazard pictured above on the 17th hole) has often decided the fate of many an Open Championship. This was the case with the two Opens played at Carnoustie in 1999 and 2007, which were won by Paul Lawrie from Scotland by Padraig Harrington from Ireland respectively.

33 bottom The 3rd hole, Jockies Burn, is the shortest par 4 on the Championship Course at Carnoustie. It is only 337 yards (308 m) long, but the water hazard, which gives the hole its name and cuts across in front of the green, prevents even great champions from aiming at the flag with their first shot.

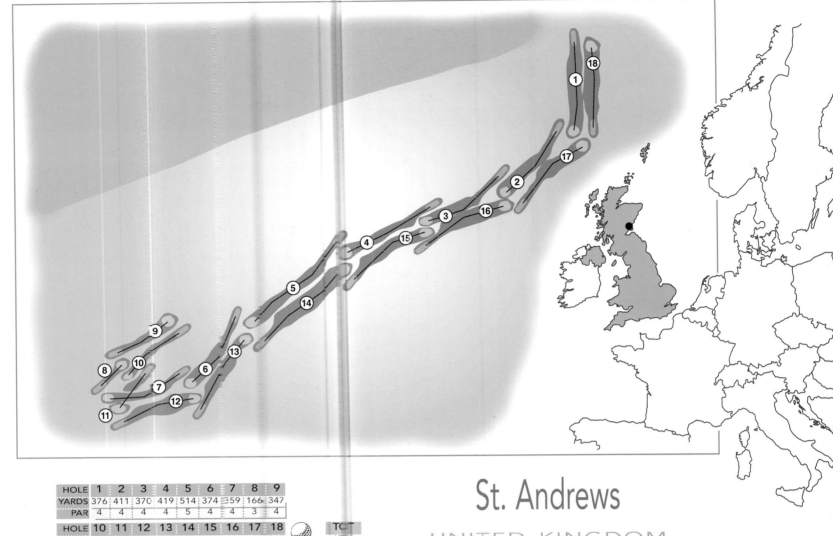

HOLE	1	2	3	4	5	6	7	8	9		
YARDS	376	411	370	419	514	374	359	166	347		
PAR	4	4	4	4	5	4	4	3	4		
HOLE	10	11	12	13	14	15	16	17	18		TOT
YARDS	340	174	316	418	530	414	381	455	357		6751
PAR	4	3	4	4	5	4	4	4	4		72

St. Andrews

UNITED KINGDOM

36 Golf has been popular in St. Andrews since the Middle Ages and the Old Course, the world's most famous course, already existed in 1764. The course complex of St. Andrews includes five 18th holes and one nine-hole, which sprawl out between the Scottish town, the sea, and the mouth of the Eden River. The seventh course, called The Castle, is southeast of the center.

37 The double greens, like the ones on the 2nd and the 16th hole, pictured right, are a characteristic of the Old Course and can be found on all holes except the 1st, the 9th, the 17th, and the 18th. The design of the course was tweaked and improved by Old Tom Morris, the most famous golfer of the 19th century.

The "home of golf." In St. Andrews, on the eastern coast of Scotland, the Game was born as a pastime for the king. Located about 56 miles (90 km) from the capital Edinburgh (the Scottish Dùn Éideann) and in the middle of the Kingdom of Fife, St. Andrews is a pleasant township, with an important history and a famous university. But today golf is definitely the main attraction of this area, with its dozen courses in an area of only a few square miles. The most important one being the legendary Old Course, the true cradle of golf and "worshipped" today by anyone who loves the game.

St. Andrews has been involved with clubs and golf balls as early as 1400 and the simple initial course, placed among pastures and sheep on the seaside, today is a perfect garden, lovingly tended by tens of employees. Each year the Old Course hosts thousands and thousands of "pilgrims" followed by great caddies who, besides carrying their bag, walk them from hole to hole, meter to meter, narrating all the history and the secrets of this course, unique for its charm and tradition.

In the Middle Ages golf was already popular in St. Andrews, to the point that in 1457 King James II was forced to forbid it because the youth preferred it to the practice of archery, much more useful to the monarch in case of war. And of all the accusations that brought Elizabeth I to behead her cousin Mary, Queen of Scots, one was that she had played golf a few days after the passing of her husband, Francis II, king of France. This is truly when the love of the game gets to someone's head. In 1764 the Old Course had 22 holes, 11 out and just as many in, back towards the clubhouse. There were actually only 12 greens because, with the exception of hole 11 and 22, the same hole was used both in and out.

The first and last four were too short and therefore they were coupled, reducing the number from 22 to today's 18, the magic number for every championship golf course. The unmistakable double greens of the Old Course are a result of the historical peculiarity that we mentioned above.

Around 1850, there was already a discreet amount of players on the course, therefore games that moved away from the clubhouse and those that moved back towards the clubhouse often 'clashed' when closing the hole. In order to avoid further problems, two separate holes were placed on each double

green, marking them with white flags (out) and red flags (in).

One of the many curious stories that the Old Course can tell us is the "rabbit war" story. In 1797, due to economic problems, the community of St. Andrews had lost the control of the course, which was partly rented out to breeders. Only 24 years later, James Cheape of Strathtyrum, a local landowner and a good player, managed to buy all the land, reserving it exclusively for golf from then on.

In the second half of the 19th century the course was improved and perfected by Old Tom Morris, the most famous golfer of his century. He created a separate green for the 1st hole, modifying the direction of the course from clockwise to counter-clockwise and arranging the 112 infamous bunker that pepper the course. Among these, the most famous is the Hell Bunker, a "monster" as big as an apartment and with a 10 ft (3 m) high bank, protecting the 14th hole. Other famous features

are the Swilcan Burn (a ditch that cuts the 1st hole in front of the green and that on the 18th is crossed by a much-photographed stone bridge) and the 17th hole, the infamous "Road Hole," on which the dreams of many Open Championship contenders were shattered. The mother of all matches was played on the Old Course at St. Andrews for the first time in 1873, and it has been hosted here a further 27 times. In recent times, it has become the main headquarters of the big event in the years that end in 0 and 5.

38 and 38-39 Tiger Woods on the tee of the 18th hole at St. Andrews, during the third round on his way to victory in the 2005 Open Championship. Right in front of him is the small stone bridge that crosses the Swilcan Burn, a water obstacle that cuts the 1st hole (right in front of the green) and the 18th hole (a few yards from the starting tees).

38-39 and 39 On the St. Andrews courses there are two clubhouses: the famous historic one, next to the tee of the 1st hole and the green of the 18th on the Old Course, and the more recent one which serves the New Course and the other links of the "home of golf."

40-41 and 40 bottom St.
Andrews is one of the oldest golf
courses. In 1764 the Old Course
had as many as 22 holes, 11 out
and 11 in towards the clubhouse.
There were only twelve greens
because, with the exception of
the 11th and the 22nd, the same
hole was used going and out.

St. Andrews

41 In the second half of the 1800s, the Old Course was improved by Old Tom Morris, the most famous golfer of the 19th century, who created a separate green for the 1st hole, modified the direction of the course from clockwise to counterclockwise and arranged the course's 112 infamous bunkers. St. Andrews also features the New Course (created in 1895), the Jubilee (1897), the Eden (1914), the Strathyrum (1993), the Castle (2008), and the easy nine holes at Balgrove.

The St. Andrews clubhouse is a wonderful piece of golf history and it is the center of the Royal & Ancient, the world's most famous club that, together with the United States Golf Association, dictates and updates the rules of the game. Founded in 1754 by 22 "noblemen and gentlemen of the Kingdom of Fife," it was first known as the Society of St. Andrews Golfers. It changed to its modern name in 1834, when King William IV granted it his patronage. Twenty years later, the modern, very famous clubhouse was built. Today the R&A has approximately 2400 members, scattered all over the world.

The Old Course is the historical gem of the most important European golf course, managed by the St. Andrews Links Trust. The other 18-hole courses are the New Course (created in 1895), Jubilee (1897), Eden (1914), and Strathyrum (1993), which adds a nine-hole course called Balgove, for neophytes and families. The latest marvelous addition is the Castle, a fascinating 18-hole course designed by David McLay Kidd, which opened in the summer of 2008. A few miles away we have the Duke's (the only inland course of the area), the two courses of St. Andrews Bay (Devlin and Torrance), and the fantastic Kingsbarns, by Kyle Phillips, which is probably the world's most beautiful modern course.

In order to sum up the charm that the Old Course exudes in two sentences we need only to quote two champions of the last 50 years: "I fell in love with it the first day I played it." Jack Nicklaus; "It is by far my favorite golf course in the world." Tiger Woods. Need we say more?

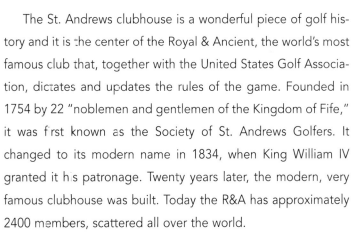

42-43 The design of the
Kingsbarns Golf Links, by the
American Kile Phillips, is simply
perfect and probably makes it
one of the most beautiful courses
built in the 21st century. The 18
holes are only a few miles south-
east of St. Andrews, along the
coast of the Firth of Fife.

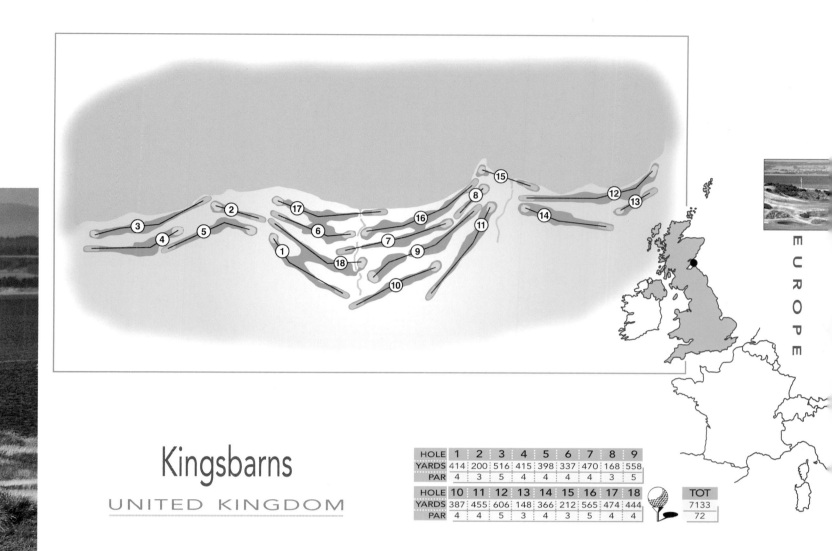

Kingsbarns

UNITED KINGDOM

HOLE	1	2	3	4	5	6	7	8	9
YARDS	414	200	516	415	398	337	470	168	558
PAR	4	3	5	4	4	4	4	3	5

HOLE	10	11	12	13	14	15	16	17	18		TOT
YARDS	387	455	606	148	366	212	565	474	444		7133
PAR	4	4	5	3	4	3	5	4	4		72

For many experts it is the best course of the 21st century. Since it was opened in 2001, Kingsbarns has represented the perfect link between the tradition of the classic Scottish links and modern golf, which on its superlative 18 holes reaches its climax. The author of this masterpiece is Kyle Phillips, the American golf-course architect who impeccably interpreted the landscape along the Firth of Fife, on the North Sea coast. Kingsbarns was born out of an idea by Mark Parsinen, a California businessman, who came to the Scottish project after previously creating two golf courses. The small town that gives its name to the course is less than 6 miles (10 km) from St. Andrews, with its seven courses, and represents a perfect completion to this extraordinary golf area.

The history of the game in Kingsbarns actually has ancient roots. In the late 18th century, the village merchants and landowners decided to form an association for the game of golf, which had already had many supporters and dedicated playing areas. In 1793 the first competitions were held during the spring and fall when medals were awarded to the best players. The vast plot of land where the holes were situated was used for golf and other leisure activities until about 1850, when the owners of the Cambo Estate decided to incorporate it into their own farm estate. It is definitely not surprising that in those days, with rare exceptions, farmland was a more profitable use of land than golf courses. It was Lady Erskine, from the Cambo Estate, who inspired the rebirth of the Kingsbarns Golfing Society after the end of the First World War.

42 bottom The clubhouse is simple but modern and functional, ideal for a course with the specifically "touristic" qualities of the Kingsbarns.

43 The course is fun, full of interesting angles, and can become impossible if played on a day with lots of wind.

Kingsbarns

Nine holes were designed by Willie Auchterlonie in the Kingsbarns Bay area. They were used until the Second World War when the land was returned to agricultural use. It was only at the end of the previous century that golf returned to Kingsbarns, to occupy that piece of land that truly seems to have been designed to be an excellent course by nature itself. The merit of Kyle Phillips' skillful design is the ability with which the Granite Bay architect successfully camouflaged his work. In fact, the course seems to have always been there, rather than having recently been created.

Another unique aspect of Kingsbarns is the presence of the sea on the horizon of nearly every hole. This was deliberately designed by Phillips in order to embellish a course that, like any respectable links, has almost no vegetation. Although a highlight is the typical, large, and impenetrable bushes that, along with formidable bunkers, are obstacles to deter the use of cautious trajectories. Making the task even more difficult are the gusts of wind, which in Scotland is an everyday occurrence. There is very little water involved, except for a couple of delicate passages and the wonderful 15th hole, a par 3 that juts out into the sea at its tip. And if the flag is placed on the right, the game is hard even for the lower handicaps, who in Kingsbarns will find the ideal terrain for an unforgettable day. But even average players will find this Scottish jewel can offer memorable moments, as long as every shot is played with great concentration and humility.

Along with the 15th hole, the signature hole described above, the other 17 should be mentioned, but in the interests of brevity we will mention only the very difficult 7th hole

44 top and center The "pot bunkers" at Kingsbarns are among the most challenging, which for years has been one of the three clubs within the Alfred Dunhill Links Championship, next to the two "legends" of the Old Course at St. Andrews and the Championship Course at Carnoustie. Even though the course is very recent (2001, the history of the game has its roots in Kingsbarns.

(a par 4 of 470 yards/430 m), the wonderful and endless 12th hole (a par 5 of 606 yards/554 m, left dogleg, following the curve of the coast) and the insidious 18th.

The last shot is very difficult, because of an entrenched stream, which is followed by the hardest green of all, which folds out on two levels and deadly slopes. One last note regarding the clubhouse is that it is simple and small, but it has all that it needs to celebrate a fabulous day of golf once you finish the 19th hole.

44 bottom The 3rd hole is an amazingly beautiful par 5, the longest among the four of the Kingsbarns. The third one, less challenging, is pictured here with actor Bill Murray, a frequent guest of the Alfred Dunhill Links Championship, an event that features champions of golf and other sports along with people from showbusiness.

44-45 One of the most fascinating aspects of Kingsbarns is the view of the sea yo get from almost every hole. The course, as any links worthy of this classification, is almost completely barren, except for the large gorse bushes scattered throughout the course.

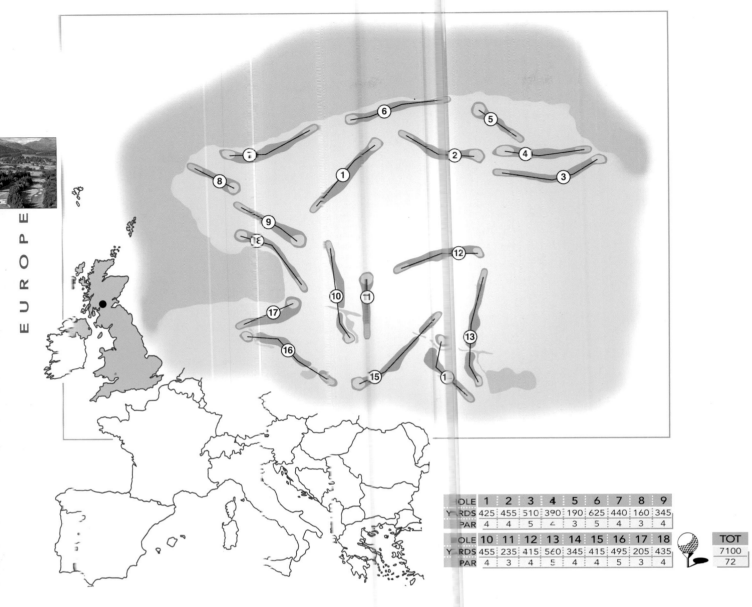

HOLE	1	2	3	4	5	6	7	8	9
YARDS	425	455	510	390	190	625	440	160	345
PAR	4	4	5	4	3	5	4	3	4

HOLE	10	11	12	13	14	15	16	17	18		TOT
YARDS	455	235	415	560	345	415	495	205	435		7100
PAR	4	3	4	5	4	4	4	3	4		72

Loch Lomond

UNITED KINGDOM

46-47 Seen from above, the greens on the 7th and the 8th holes surround the majestic Rossdhu House at Loch Lomond. The clubhouse of this exclusive Scottish club, located at the center of a 667 acre (270 hectare) estate, is a building of history and charm, which has paintings and furniture from the 18th century.

A piece of dreamland, Loch Lomond is a gem in the heart of Scotland. About half an hour northwest of Glasgow, this extraordinary course rests on the lush shores of a loch which by day is incredibly blue but often turns nasty when the strong winds of these latitudes start to blow. Loch Lomond, a private and exclusive club, has one of the most fascinating course parklands in the world. The 18 holes designed by Tom Weiskopf and Jay Morrish has hosted several Scottish Opens, becoming its de facto headquarters. Over 7100 yards (6500 m) set in parkland and opened in 1994, this immensely beautiful par 72 is played through forests and along the lake shore. Golf Digest ranked it 11th among the Best Courses Outside the United States, and the British magazine Golf World ranked it the best inland course in Britain. Furthermore, Bunkered, the only Scottish golf magazine, even gave it the title of No. 1 course in Scotland, ahead of the likes of St. Andrews, Turnberry, Muirfield, and Carnoustie. This is definitely enough to underline the importance of Loch Lomond, a gorgeous 18-hole.

Complex, challenging, full of natural obstacles, the course is slightly meandering and is spectacularly framed by trees. Naturally, the most scenic holes are the ones facing the lake (5th, 6th, and 7th). The 18th's approach is unforgettable. This par 4 is overlooked by the ruins of Castle Rossdhu, a fortress that rises above the green where in the 16th century Queen Mary wrote her famous love letters. Each hole has a name, a charming custom at every important British course. The club is in the middle of a 667 acre (270 hectare) estate that belonged to the Colquhoun Clan, who also built the superb Rossdhu House, which today has been converted into a fabulous clubhouse rich with history and charm.

In order to broaden what it had to offer, in 2003 the club acquired Dundonald, a masterpiece by Kyle Phillips, an American architect who has also created the magnificent Kingsbarns course, about 6 miles (10 km) from St. Andrews. Not too far from Troon, in Ayrshire, and an hour by car from Loch Lomond, Dundonald is about a drive shot from the sea and with its 7330 yards (6700 m), this links is a delight for true golf connoisseurs. In contrast to Loch Lomond, which is rigorously reserved for members and their guests, at Dundonald it is possible for outsiders to book tee time.

47 bottom In the past few years Loch Lomond has become the fixed venue for the Scottish Open, the most important competition in the country, second only to the Open Championship when, by rotation, it takes place in Scotland. The exceptional 18-hole course, a parkland of rare beauty, is the work of Tom Weiskopf and Jay Morrish.

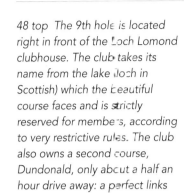

48 top The 9th hole is located right in front of the Loch Lomond clubhouse. The club takes its name from the lake (loch in Scottish) which the beautiful course faces and is strictly reserved for members, according to very restrictive rules. The club also owns a second course, Dundonald, only about a half an hour drive away: a perfect links designed by the famous American architect Kyle Phillips.

48 center and bottom In these two photographs is the green on the 18th an aerial view of the Loch Lomond course. The club's park also features the ruins of Rossdhu Castle, which dates back to the 16th century. Queen Mary, who was one of the first women keen on golf, penned a few love letters in this castle.

Next to the amazing 18 holes designed by Weiskopf and Morrish, another course is being created at Loch Lomond, which will complete the club's portfolio, making it truly unique in the world. The design of this course has been assigned to the great Jack Nicklaus, who has promised to create a veritable work of art, with many holes facing the lake shore.

Rossdhu House, Loch Lomond's clubhouse, was refurbished in 1997. As far as size and the refinement of its interiors it is probably unparalleled in the world. There are two large dining rooms with high ceilings: Scottish fabrics with maroon and blue tones for the smaller room, the Clan room, and lighter colors (green and beige) for the other room, with large windows facing the 8th hole and the lake. Then there is the Rossdhu Bar, with an endless choice of liqueurs and whiskies, including the fine Loch Lomond whisky (a delicate 12-year unblended), the large library, drawing room, and a conference hall. Big 18th-century canvases decorate the interiors, with ancient armchairs and couches dominating the rooms, while antiques, precious books, and majestic draperies complete the charming decor. On the second floor there are six suites in different styles, while on the main floor is the informal Spike Bar, the well-supplied pro shop, and the comfortable dressing rooms with blue carpeting and Scottish patterns, large leather couches, and mahogany lockers.

Scattered throughout the park and holes are small cottages housing about 40 apartments for members and their lucky guests, all decorated with luxurious and refined details. In the middle of the resort we have a sumptuous and extremely modern spa, which borders a large winter garden enclosed by tall, ancient walls. The last surprise in this corner of heaven.

48-49 The 7th hole, is one of the most spectacular holes at Loch Lomond, along with the 5th and 6th.

49 bottom The spectacular green on the 18th at Loch Lomond during a round in the Scottish Open, a tournament that for years has permanently been hosted at the beautiful Dunbartonshire club.

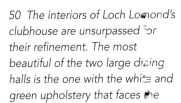

50 The interiors of Loch Lomond's clubhouse are unsurpassed for their refinement. The most beautiful of the two large dining halls is the one with the white and green upholstery that faces the front part of the Rossdhu House. The bar, one of the suites, and the exceptional men's dressing room give a partial idea of the impeccable style that dominates the clubhouse.

50-51 and 51 bottom
The drawing room with its splendid fireplace and 18th-century pairtings, exemplifies the nobility that permeates Possdhu House, which once belonged to the Colquhoun Clan and was renovated in 1997. More recently, a large spa opened in an area that also features a greenhouse and a winter garden. The estate also has various lodges for members and their guests.

Loch Lomond

54-55 *From the terraces of the 13th hole the crowd watches Jay Haas (U.S.) attempting to exit the (grass-padded) pot bunker in the final round of the 2007 Senior Open Championship.*

54 bottom *The green of the 13th hole is one of the most beautiful par 3s of the Open Championship: uphill, with five super-deep bunkers fiercely defending the narrow green, tilted on the front.*

Muirfield

55 Starting from the 1st hole, one gets a taste of what follows: countless bunkers, many of which are small yet deep and padded with grass (the so-called pot bunkers), which punish bad fairway shots and make the approach to the green very difficult; the tall thick rough in which it is advisable not to end up in; and small greens, raised and with several inclinations (in front, in the back, laterally), which are particularly problematic on the final putt. But all this makes Muirfield the ideal course.

The superstars of yesterday and today classify Muirfield as the most loyal of the historical courses in Great Britain. "Cruelly loyal," was how Henry Cotton described it. In fact, though it is a deadly test, with its narrow and long fairways and its rolling and fast greens, it does not hide its obstacles, not even its bunkers, and it lacks any bumps and knolls. There is only one blind shot: the 11th hole, a par 4 of 385 yards (352 m) with its green surrounded by deep bunkers. "There is not one weak hole," claimed Tom Watson. Donald Steel, famed architect and president of the English Golf Union, declared: "Ask a dozen golfers to classify courses and you will get as many different answers but over Muirfield there is absolute unanimity… one thing over which few will argue is that Muirfield embraces more of the qualities that a perfectionist seeks in his ideal course."

From the very 1st hole, a par 4 of 447 yards (409 m), you get the feeling of things to come on the rest of the course. One of the course's countless large bunkers occupies the left part of the narrow fairway and if you make a mistake, the rough poses a serious problem, and the green is back-sloped. The major challenge in Muirfield, however, is probably the four par 3s, with their small raised greens, protected by deep bunkers. The 188 yard (172 m) 16th, for example, is a minefield with seven bunkers and an inclination that makes the ball roll into them if the shot slightly deviates to the left. Precision and shot accuracy are necessary for all the holes of this course, which from the championship tees measures 6975 yards (6377 m). You will also need a lot of patience to book tee time because guests can only play two days a week, with tee-offs limited to a couple of hours.

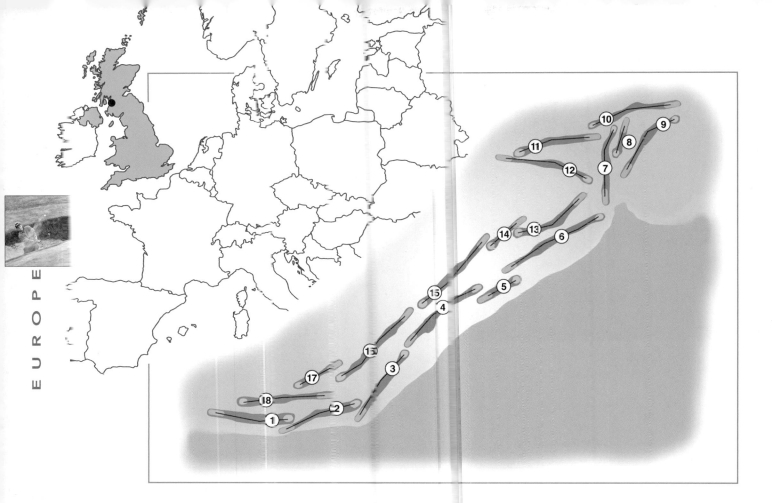

Royal Troon

UNITED KINGDOM

HOLE	1	2	3	4	5	6	7	8	9
YARDS	361	390	379	558	210	601	402	122	423
PAR	4	4	4	5	3	5	4	3	4

HOLE	10	11	12	13	14	15	16	17	18	TOT
YARDS	437	488	431	470	178	481	541	221	453	7146
PAR	4	4	4	4	3	4	5	3	4	71

One of the great, classic courses, where golf is played in its purest form. It is no wonder that the magnificent Old Course in Troon was given "Royal" status. This Scottish course became a member of the exclusive circle of British clubs proud to include "Royal" in their names in 1978 when it was celebrating its first century of existence.

Situated on the coast of the Firth of Clyde, halfway between Glasgow and that other golf jewel, Turnberry, the club looks out towards the Irish Sea, the island of Arran, and the long shape of the Mull of Kintyre. As one of the courses in the British Open Championship rotation, the Old Course has had the honor of hosting the event eight times: 1923, 1950, 1962, 1973, 1982, 1989, 1997, 2004. Today, it is part of a group of six courses that surround the county of Ayrshire, of which it is by far the most famous. Troon Golf Club was founded in 1878 on 16th March, when a group of enthusiasts gathered at the Portland Arms Hotel to announce its creation and the first captain was James Dickie. It took some time to develop the course, however, and two years later there were still only six holes available for the members. The course eventually had 12 holes and was completed by George Strath in 1888, when it was "3 miles, 1 furlong (an imperial measurement that equals 1/8 of a mile) and 156 yards" long, which was slightly more than 5685 yards (5200 m). The present-day course is more than 7100 yards (6500 m). Other important adjustments to the course's design were carried out by Willie Ferrie in the late 19th century. In 1895, the second course was inaugurated and was called Relief until 1924, when it became Portland.

56 The 1st hole of Royal Troon is an easy straight par 4 of 361 yards (330 m), with its green protected by five bunkers. It stretches out next to the sea, along the Firth of Clyde. It is not unusual to see a seal resting on the rocks not too far from the beach, which is why this hole is called Seal.

57 Craigend is the name of the 18th hole, which was the name of an old farm that no longer exists. The grand finale of the round features an excellent par 4 of 453 yards (414 m). This part also requires an eye for bunkers, which tightly surround the green, closed off in the back by an out of bounds.

58 bottom left The first par 3 at Royal Troon is the placid Greenan (the 5th hole), which is reminiscent of the ruins of Castle Kennedy not too far away. The most famous is the 8th, the Postage Stamp, known as such because of its stamp-sized green. Considered the easiest of the round, it is actually a par 3 that has made life tough for more than one champion during the Open Championships held here.

58-59 and 58 bottom right There are only three par 5s at Royal Troon, which consequently makes it a par 71. The first par 5 is the 4th, an interesting right dogleg of 558 yards (510 m). In 1838, the 18-hole course was only about 5687 yards (5200 m), which in 2004, during the last Open Championship, became 7146 yards (6537 m).

Royal Troon

The Old Course in Troon is a links par excellence, with no trees on the whole course and always swept by the wind, which is strong. The wind is the golfer's greatest adversary, as it often blows sideways on the fairways. Even the design is typical of an old Scottish course, with the holes gradually moving away from the clubhouse till the green of the 9th hole. From the tee of the 10th the course then returns to the starting point. The course begins quite obligingly, but yard after yard it becomes harder. By the turning point it has become an awesome links, with the inward nine being among the hardest in the world. If you really wanted to find a defect in this practically perfect course, you might mention Prestwick airport, which is only ten minutes by car from here. It is great for the connections but a bit too noisy, because the planes often fly low over players' heads. A further nuisance (though minor in comparison) is the railroad on the right of the inward holes.

The Royal Troon's repertoire of hazards includes many deep bunkers to be avoided at all costs, and tough greens that must be carefully analyzed. The greens are always superbly maintained, as is the whole course. Of the many great holes, particular mention must be made of the longest one, the endless 601 yards (550 m) of the 6th, known as Turnberry, and the hardest one, the 11th (The Railway), a terrible par 4 of 488 yards (446 m). The most famous hole is the also the shortest, the 8th, which is only 122 yards (112 m) and is known as the Postage Stamp. Considering its length, it is the shortest hole played in the British Open Championship, one wouldn't believe it to be so tough. However, there are five extremely deep bunkers around the long yet narrow green, which make life hard even for the best players. For example, the great Walter Hagen lost the 1923 Open Championship, after getting stuck in one. The 8th hole can also offer great satisfaction, as it did for the 71-year old Gene Sarazen in 1973. Forty-one years after winning the Open at Prince's Golf Club, Sandwich, he managed to close the Postage Stamp in one shot with a 5 iron. Quite satisfying indeed.

59 top The Englishman Luke Donald is pictured here trying to get out of one of the bunkers of the 8th hole, the Postage Stamp. Not an easy feat, considering the height of the banks and the small size of the green.

59 bottom Even Greg Norman had to challenge the "burns" (streams) found scattered here and there on Scottish links. Here, the champ is trying to fish the ball out of the 16th, the only par 5 on the back nine.

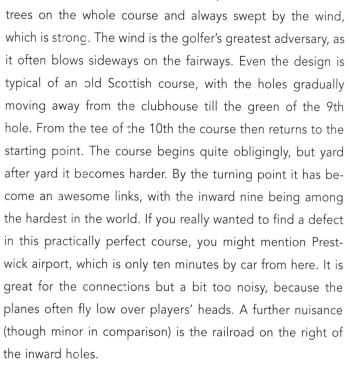

HOLE	1	2	3	4	5	6	7	8	9
YARDS	350	430	462	164	442	231	529	431	453
PAR	4	4	4	3	4	3	5	4	4

HOLE	10	11	12	13	14	15	16	17	18		TOT
YARDS	452	174	446	412	449	209	409	497	431		6974
PAR	4	3	4	4	4	3	4	5	4		70

Turnberry

UNITED KINGDOM

I t is said that Turnberry is the Pebble Beach of the British Isles, but could it be the other way around? Turnberry was created first, in 1902, 13 years before its American counterpart, and like all Scottish links it has that almost completely natural atmosphere often lacking overseas. Whatever one may think Turnberry combines views and two championship courses, one of them legendary, the Ailsa, for a mix that makes it one of the favorite golfing centers in Scotland and abroad.

The Ailsa, one of the most scenic courses the Open Championship has ever been played on, was made famous by the hard-fought dual in 1977 between Jack Nicklaus and Tom Watson, who won by a stroke. This match went down in history as the "Duel in the Sun," a name that was then given to the 18th hole. Another great moment was the amazing second round by Greg Norman in the 1986 Open, who, despite the storm and a final triple putt finale finished in 63, a score that still today is considered one of the best scores in the history of the Open. And not forgetting the victory putt by Nick Price in 1996, on the 17th hole – 50 ft (15 m) for an eagle.

The view at Turnberry is another strong point: the impressive Ailsa Craig – a granite massif that stands 11 miles (18 km) off the coast – the island of Arran, the mysterious Mull of Kintyre (made famous by a Paul McCartney song), everything contributes to distract the player. Even the hotel on the hill, which sparkles like a diamond in the sunset, is a trademark. When it was opened, four years after the course was, it had a covered passage that connected it to the station so that guests would not get wet during the walk.

60 and 60-61 The resort's five-star Westin Turnberry Hotel also features a spa per for wellness treatments. Since the hotel opened in the early 20th century, the view has remained virtually untouched all the way to the beach and Ailsa Craig.

61 bottom The 17th is a short par 3 that plays out on the dunes. The Ailsa Course made the headlines thanks to the epic dual between Jack Nicklaus and Tom Watson during the 1977 Open, which went down in history as the "Duel in the Sun."

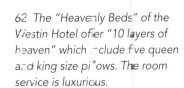

Turnberry

62 The "Heavenly Beds" of the Westin Hotel offer "10 layers of heaven" which include five queen and king size pillows. The room service is luxurious.

62–63, 63 top left and bottom A perfect venue for conferences, Turnberry even has 14 event halls of various capacities to choose

from. The rooms can host meetings and group luncheons, as well as a private and comfortable dinner.

63 top right Boiseries, antique paintings decorate the walls of the stairway that leads to the upper floor.

63 center Comfortable and spacious lounges where you can sit down and have a drink or read a book and relax.

65 top Besides the natural dunes that characterize the links and the rocky aras that plummet down to sea, there are also many bunkers to shake things up on this course.

65 bottom About 65 yards (60 m) from the green of the 10th hole, a downhill par 4, is the most fearsome bunker at Ailsa: a large circle of sand with a grass island in the middle.

64-65 The land that is home to Turnberry went from being railway property more than 100 years ago to an air base during the two World Wars, but has always been a natural links from day one.

64 bottom left The green of the 16th is surrounded by a deep water course, the Wilson Burn. To reach it, players must cross a small wooden bridge.

64 bottom right The monument for the fallen soldiers gives the 12th hole of the Ailsa Corse its name, Monument: a par 4 that can compromise a good score.

Turnberry

Turnberry risked extinction twice. During both World Wars it was turned into an air base, and during the Second World War concrete (still visible as a reminder of those dark days) replaced several holes. The course survived only thanks to the endurance of the owners and the efforts of Philip Mackenzie Ross, who after two years of hard work managed to reopen the links in 1951.

The first holes introduce the player to the difficulties that will follow, especially when the wind blows from Ailsa Craig. But it is on the tee of the 4th, 164 yards (150 m) from the violently flapping flag on the tiny green on the rocks, that players truly realize that they are playing by the Irish Sea, some 37 miles (60 km) south of Glasgow. From the 4th to the 11th the first five are surrounded by dunes and the last holes by rocky cliffs.

A succession of holes that offers a fascinating experience and requires solid, powerful shots; only the best players come out of it with their pride unscathed. The 9th is the most remarkable, a par 4 of 453 yards (415 m) called Bruce's Castle. The tee

shot from the high promontory on the sea may be a blind shot, but the player in front of the lighthouse and the ruins of the castle of Robert the Bruce (Scottish king, 1306–29) is not: it is hard to stay concentrated on the game, and maximum concentration is needed here. Just reaching the tee can be a shaky experience, and trying not to lose balance during the swing, when the wind is strong, is quite a feat.

The 16th is equally famous and is called the Wee Burn, a par 4 of 409 yards (374 m). The drive must be at least 249 yards (228 m) to allow a decent approach. The green is surrounded by the Wilson Burn and the balls that do not fully land in the green risk rolling into the depth of its waters (in order to retrieve a ball there are long poles provided).

The locals say that if you can see Ailsa Craig, it is about to rain, and if you can not, it is already raining. This typical British humor is sometimes contradicted by days that are so sunny that you can see Ireland in the distance. Otherwise what Duel in the Sun would there have been during the 1977 Open?

66-67 The lighthouse at Turnberry makes the 9th hole unmistakable. It was named Bruce Castle for the nearby ruins of the castle that belonged to the famous Scottish king of the 14th century.

67 top From the green of the 6th you can see the lighthouse of the 9th. It is the longest par 3 of the course 231 yards (211 m). From the tee you can clearly see the menacing bunkers guarding the green. On the right is the fairway of the 17th.

67 bottom Dave Edward (U.S.) is tackling a bunker defending the green of the 6th hole during the 2006 Senior British Open.

Turnberry

68-69 From this aerial picture you can see the 9th, 14th, and 18th holes that fan out from and converge on the clubhouse. The 18th is one of the most famous final holes in Britain. If the drive lands slightly on the right, the approach to the green is difficult. A keen choice of clubs can close with a birdie.

68 bottom The Art Deco clubhouse dominates the green of the 18th and from the enormous windows you can see most of the course. The original clubhouse, which dates back to 1897, was rebuilt in 1904 and in 1935 it was replaced with the present-day one, which was refurbished for the 1961 Open Championship.

69 The 4th hole is the first par 3, the longest of the four. It has a raised tee and a green well protected by bunkers.

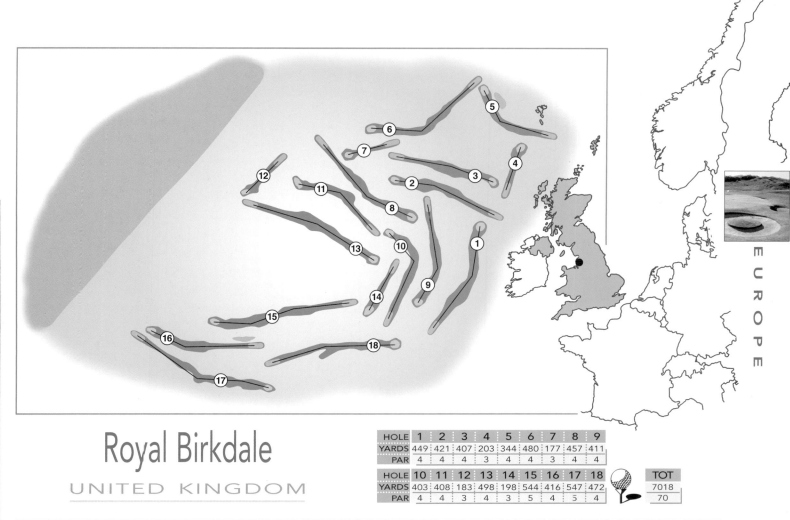

Royal Birkdale

UNITED KINGDOM

HOLE	1	2	3	4	5	6	7	8	9
YARDS	449	421	407	203	344	480	177	457	411
PAR	4	4	4	3	4	4	3	4	4

HOLE	10	11	12	13	14	15	16	17	18		TOT
YARDS	403	408	183	498	198	544	416	547	472		7018
PAR	4	4	3	4	3	5	4	5	4		70

A good indication of the greatness of the Royal Birkdale is the number of events that it has hosted. Besides the Curtis Cup, Walker Cup, two Ryder Cups and the Women's British Open, it is one of the clubs in the Open Championship rotation. From 1954 to 1998 it has hosted eight Opens, and it will host it again in 2008. Birkdale was born in 1889 as a nine-hole course in Shaw Hills. An unusual moment of progressive thought resulted in the members of the club unanimously voting in favor of allowing ladies to use the links, an incredible development for that time and place, even if it was only "for three days a week and not more, and not on Saturday and Bank Holiday."

In 1894 the course was expanded and moved to Birkdale Hills, but it took three years for everyone to be convinced the right choice had been made. In fact, many feared that golf was a passing fad, comparable to the temporary craze for table tennis. The 18 holes designed by George Low were therefore inaugurated in 1897, but the status of championship course was only achieved in the 1930s, when it was redesigned and improved by F.W. Hawtree (a golf-course architect) and J.H. Taylor (who dominated the Open Championship in the 20 years before the First World War). They applied the theory that made holes run flat through the dunes instead of directly on them. The final consecration took place in 1951, when King George VI bestowed the Royal to its name.

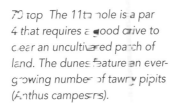

70 top The 11th hole is a par 4 that requires a good drive to clear an uncultivated patch of land. The dunes feature an ever-growing number of tawny pipits (Anthus campestris).

70 bottom A bunker with a central flower bed on the 7th hole. In general, greens are protected by pot bunkers, whose walls are tall and vertical and are deeper than the common bunker.

Royal Birkdale

The course, situated on the coast of the Irish Sea, a few miles north of Liverpool, enjoys the rightful reputation of being a difficult yet honest test, with the tees generally offering a good view of the hole. Straight shots are well rewarded, while botched shots are punished by thorny bushes and dwarf willows. It is a beautiful course to play and to look at, and its high dunes to the sides of the fairway offer natural bleachers for spectators. After the 1991 Open Championship the bold and expensive choice was made to completely reconstruct all

the greens, which still today are difficult to figure out, thus allowing the Royal Birkdale to continue to be one of the best links in the world.

There is no shortage of beautiful holes here. One of the most famous ones is the 15th, the longest and hardest par 5, with its narrow fairway and its 15 bunkers to deal with. A plate commemorates the incredible shot made by Arnold Palmer in terrible weather conditions on his way to victory in the 1961 Open. The 18th hole is one of the country's most famous final holes, in which the approach to the green can be hindered by the tendency to drive slightly to the right. The green is well protected by three bunkers, but a shrewd choice of clubs can end a good golfer's match with a birdie.

For the 2008 Open, Royal Birkdale underwent a series of alterations to keep the course user-friendly – as described by Peter Thompson after his victory in the 1965 Open – even though new challenges were installed for contemporary world champions. Martin Hawtree maintained somewhat of a family tradition by designing the alterations, with a mere 153 yard (140 m) increase, for a total length of 7018 yards (6417 m). The green of the 17th was also redesigned and 16 new bunkers and 6 tees were added. These tees offer more strategic solutions for the first shot. One of the obstacles that everyone must face, from whichever tee they start, is the wind. For average players this can even mean difficulty in reaching the fairway with the drive.

Finally, a particular aspect that makes Royal Birkdale a unique place is the variety of flora and fauna, due to the topography of the dunes. A guide has been compiled for players providing a description of the species they may encounter during a round.

70-71 Royal Birkdale is not only beautiful to play, but also to look at: the tall dunes on the edge of the fairway double as natural bleachers for spectators.

71 bottom The pot bunkers guarding the greens leave little margin for error, supported by the defensive role of the dunes and rough areas of grass and flowers.

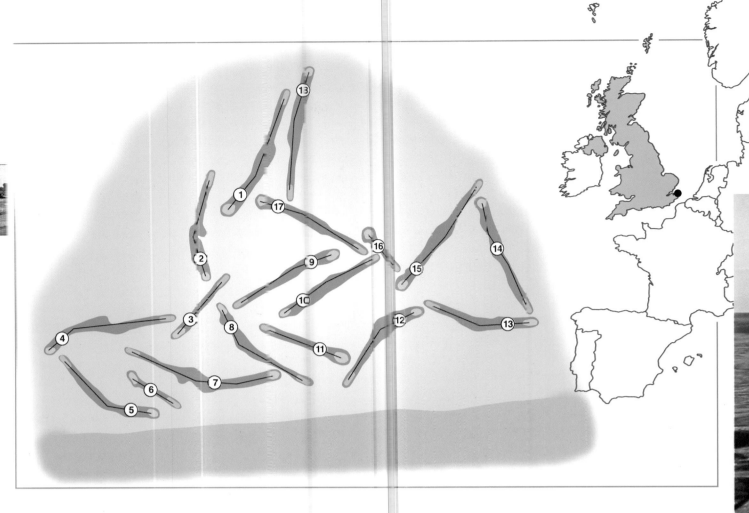

HOLE	1	2	3	4	5	6	7	8	9
YARDS	440	416	208	495	418	170	530	453	346
PAR	4	4	3	4	4	3	5	4	–

HOLE	10	11	12	13	14	15	16	17	18	TOT
YARDS	412	240	379	457	548	473	161	426	4 8	7070
PAR	4	3	4	4	5	4	3	4	–	70

Royal St. George's
UNITED KINGDOM

Like many truly important links, Royal St. George's was created almost by chance in 1887 when the Scotsman William Laidlaw Purves started looking for a piece of land that would be suitable to build a course for Londoners, who were forced to use crowded courses that were often poorly maintained. In Sandwich, southeast of the capital, he stumbled upon a huge dune formation and decided it was just the place. Named St. George's after the English patron saint, in 1902 it was given Royal status by King Edward VII.

If golf is a game that forces man to reinvent himself according to the course and to the situation, Royal St. George's has endured the same fate because since its birth it has regenerated several times in order to adapt to the new playing techniques, without ever sacrificing its original purpose. This is how it maintained its reputation of being the "English St. Andrews," one of the most difficult links to host an Open. It has hosted 13 Open Championship in the 110 years of its existence, from 1894 (the first time it crossed the Scottish border) to 2003, and is ready to do so again in 2011. It remains in this important group of courses partly due to the abundance of space that allows it to lengthen the holes and to keep up with the modern game. The fairways are never parallel and change direction constantly, an important factor for when there is wind, which there almost always is.

Opinions on the Sandwich course are decidedly varied. Many Tour players dislike it, but many Tour reporters adore it. All depends on what is meant by a 'great' course. You either want a course that shows all its obstacles so that you know exactly how

72 The 14th hole is probably the most famous, with an out of bounds along the whole right side with the canal crossing the fairway 328 yards (300 m) from the tee.

72-73 A par 3, the 6th hole is cheekily nicknamed Maiden because the dunes between the 5th and the 6th make it look like a maiden lying down.

73 bottom Standing on the tee of the 1st hole is like entering history. During its 110 years of life, the Royal St. George's has hosted 13 Open Championships. The 14th will be held on this English links – considered among the hardest of courses to host this tournament – in 2011.

74-75 A different setting for the 5th hole. The two-tiered green is surrounded by four bunkers: the right choice of clubs is essential, especially in the presence of wind.

74 bottom The enormous bunker in front of the green of the 4th hole seems, and is, very menacing. Once avoided or cleared, you will be in front of the green, which dangerously slopes to out of bounds.

75 Among the courses that rotate in the Open Championship, the Royal St. George's is considered to be one of the hardest, together with Carnoustie. The large number of bunkers vary in shape but not in size, and are never the size of the ones across the ocean.

to face it, or you believe the game is not amusing enough without some blind shots or without golf balls bouncing into the rough. In any case, nobody expects it to be an easy course. The Open Championship course is not supposed to be easy at all, but Royal St. George's is considered the most difficult of all, except possibly for Carnoustie. One can understand the fact that only three Open winners here – Bill Rogers in 1981, Greg Norman in 1993, and Ben Curtis in 2003 – managed to finish four under par.

As mentioned, in order to continue to host the Open, the course has had to go through various modifications. This offers an interesting study on the development of golf architecture over the course of a century. For example, the end of the gutta-percha golf balls demanded transformations before hosting the 1911 Open. Later on, there was a need to better balance the length of the holes out and in. Blind shots were no longer fashionable after the Second World War and the course fell into disgrace until the mid-1970s, when further modifications were

made. This was one of the reasons why it did not host the Open once between 1949 and 1981. Every hole of this course is different and each one is difficult. The hardest one by definition – Stroke Index 1 – is the 8th hole, which was transformed in 1975 by Pennink from a par 3 into a formidable par 4 of 453 yards (416 m) with an uphill drive and a dogleg to the right. The second shot must fly over a wide area of rough before landing on a long, undulating green surrounded by dunes. The 10th is famous not only because it is the most dangerous par 4 in England (in the 1993 Open it featured 16 double bogeys or worse) but also because Ian Fleming made it the location for a match between James Bond and Goldfinger, even though in the book the club is called Royal St. Mark's.

Royal St. George's

76-77 The Royal Porthcawl is unanimously considered the best Welsh golf club. The club's incorporation dates back to about 1891, when it was founded by some businessmen from Cardiff involved in the coal industry.

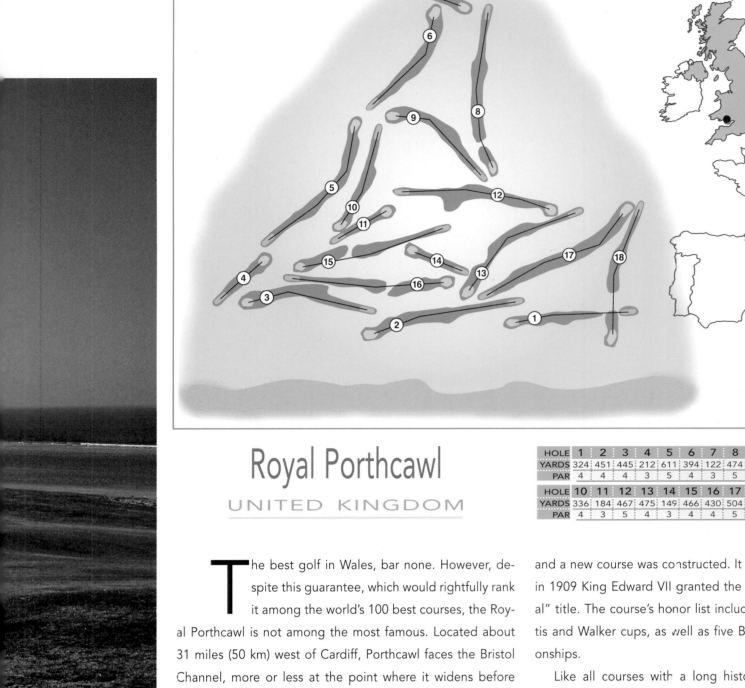

Royal Porthcawl

UNITED KINGDOM

HOLE	1	2	3	4	5	6	7	8	9		
YARDS	324	451	445	212	611	394	122	474	375		
PAR	4	4	4	3	5	4	3	5	4		

HOLE	10	11	12	13	14	15	16	17	18		TOT
YARDS	336	184	467	475	149	466	430	504	410		6829
PAR	4	3	5	4	3	4	4	5	4		72

The best golf in Wales, bar none. However, despite this guarantee, which would rightfully rank it among the world's 100 best courses, the Royal Porthcawl is not among the most famous. Located about 31 miles (50 km) west of Cardiff, Porthcawl faces the Bristol Channel, more or less at the point where it widens before flowing into the Irish Sea. Once a land of coal mines, Wales was one of the world's biggest exporters of coal, with Cardiff as the main port. In this region golf really established itself in the late 19th century. The Welsh Golfing Union was founded in 1895 and nine years later even women created their own association.

The Porthcawl Golf Club existed already, as demonstrated by its certificate of incorporation of 1891. Some Cardiff businessmen, who became wealthy by trading coal and had a fondness for the game, found an ideal seaside site near Porthcawl (in those days it was a moderately important port). In less than a year the founders obtained the rights to model fairways and greens for nine holes, but several months were needed to strip the land of the thick gorse bushes and ferns. At the end of the clearing process a professional was hired from Westward Ho! (also known as Royal North Devon), the oldest golf club in England, which was founded in 1864. His name was Charles Gibson and he laid out the original nine holes in 1892. Only three years later the club was moved to its present-day site, where the course was expanded to 18 holes. In just a few seasons the first course was abandoned

and a new course was constructed. It was such a success that in 1909 King Edward VII granted the club the coveted "Royal" title. The course's honor list includes hosting several Curtis and Walker cups, as well as five British Amateur Championships.

Like all courses with a long history, Porthcawl has also been progressively improved and refined, while always maintaining the style of a traditional links.

76 bottom The course in Porthcawl is not very long (6829 yards/6244 m) and does not feature water hazards or trees.

77 The 18 holes in Porthcawl are about 31 miles (50 km) west of the Welsh capital, Cardiff. The "Royal" was awarded to the club by King Edward VII in 1909.

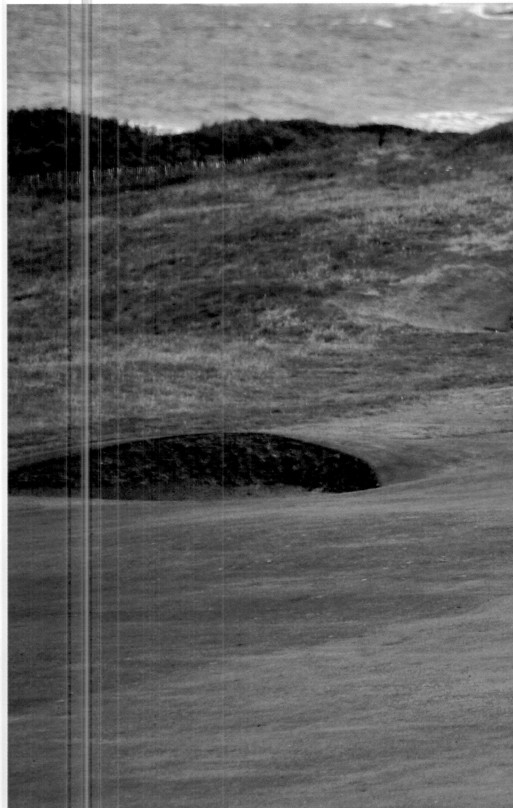

The first important contribution to this process was made by Harry Colt in 1913, followed 20 years later by Tom Simpson. Royal Porthcawl differs from other links in a few technical characteristics. There are no typical sandy dunes, allowing endless views. The holes do not follow one another according to a precise pattern, and take different directions that are apparently uncoordinated. This allows the wind to modify its influence at every shot, forcing players to choose their clubs with extreme care. Another differing aspect is the type

of terrain. If the first four and the last six holes are perfect links without any obstacles except for the bunker, the intermediate ones are closer to the concept of "heathland," or terrain with a lot of bushes acting as deadly traps. The middle holes are in a raised area, a wide plateau that offers magnificent views of the Bristol Channel and the Glamorgan Coast.

Royal Porthcawl is not one of the longest courses (6829 yards/6244 m) and it has no water obstacles or trees. But its bunkers and bushes are more than enough to protect the course, especially when the breeze is replaced by a stiff wind that blows from the Atlantic. Among the holes that deserve a mention is the 9th, a difficult par 4 with a green protected by five tremendous pot bunkers. The clubhouse is pleasant and comfortable, and it mirrors the overall relaxed and informal atmosphere of the club. Just one more reason to test your skills at this superb gem, the great pride of Welsh golf, on a par with Celtic Manor, Newport (host of the 2010 Ryder Cup).

79 bottom The many deep bunkers are more than enough to protect the flags with the aid of the strong wind blowing from the Atlantic, which is so close it touches almost four of the course's holes.

78 and 78-79 The intriguing course of the Royal Porthcawl Golf Club. The Club was inaugurated in 1891. It hasn't water hazards or trees.

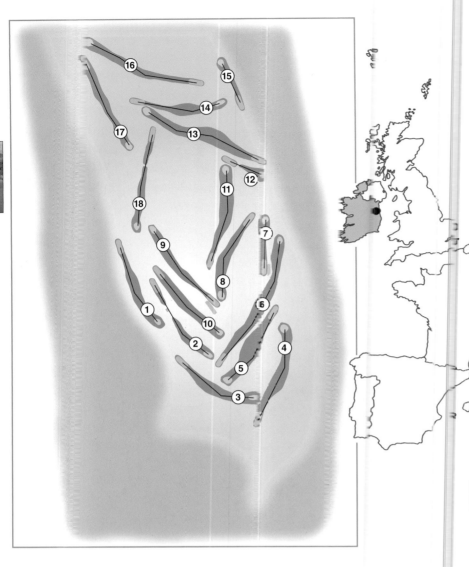

HOLE	1	2	3	4	5	6	7	8	9
YARDS	405	411	398	474	442	603	184	426	437
PAR	4	4	4	4	4	5	3	4	4

HOLE	10	11	12	13	14	15	16	17	18		TOT
YARDS	370	428	160	565	411	190	577	472	411		7364
PAR	4	4	3	5	4	3	5	4	4		72

80 and 8 *bottom* The clubhouse in Portmarnock was completely refurbished recently at a cost of about five million euros. The first nine holes of the club were opened on the 26th December 1894, while the course, divided into the Blue and Red course, was completed two years later.

80-81 *The Portmarnock Golf Club, a few miles north of Dublin, is one of the best courses in Ireland. From its fairways there are superb views of the two small islands, Ireland's Eye and Lambay.*

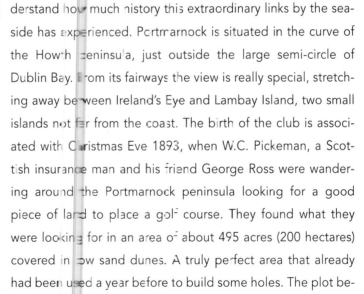

Portmarnock

IRELAND

A handful of miles north of Dublin is Portmarnock Golf Club, a golf legend in Ireland. You just need to know that it was created in 1894 to understand how much history this extraordinary links by the seaside has experienced. Portmarnock is situated in the curve of the Howth peninsula, just outside the large semi-circle of Dublin Bay. From its fairways the view is really special, stretching away between Ireland's Eye and Lambay Island, two small islands not far from the coast. The birth of the club is associated with Christmas Eve 1893, when W.C. Pickeman, a Scottish insurance man and his friend George Ross were wandering around the Portmarnock peninsula looking for a good piece of land to place a golf course. They found what they were looking for in an area of about 495 acres (200 hectares) covered in low sand dunes. A truly perfect area that already had been used a year before to build some holes. The plot belonged to the Jameson family, also of Scottish origin, who had already become wealthy thanks to their distillery, one of Dublin's two alcohol-related dynasties, the other being the Guinness family.

Fortunately, all concerned were golfers and so it was easy for Pickeman to negotiate a 25-year rent at a courtesy price. John Jameson was nominated first president of the Portmarnock Golf Club and Pickeman chose the role of Secretary and Honorary Treasurer, while Ross became Captain. The inauguration of the first nine holes occurred rather quickly, considering the comparatively untouched state of the terrain, and was followed a year later by the first expansion on 26th December, 1894.

82-83 and 82 bottom The course of the Portmarnock Golf Club is extremely rigorous, which has rightfully put it amongst the world's top ten courses of this kind. The greens are often very large and protected by tough bunkers. Slightly to the north, is its "cousin" the Portmarnock Golf Links, which is an excellent 18-hole course.

83 top Since 1971 a respectable third course (Yellow) was added to the orginal 18 holes of the Portmarnock club. This course is located slightly north of the Howth Peninsula, which closes off the northern part of Dublin Bay.

83 center and bottom The historic Portmarnock Golf Club has a gorgeous clubhouse, simple and almost austere in style, perfectly matching the impeccable design of the course.

Portmarnock

A few seasons passed before the project was completed, bringing the course up to 18 holes by the end of 1896. In 1971, next to the Red and Blue courses that comprise the championship course, the excellent nine-hole Yellow course was created.

As with all true links, the wind is the great leveller and can transform a difficult yet honest course like Portmarnock into a true nightmare. The 18 holes can become diabolical to play when gusts of wind sweep the coast, easily carrying the ball off into a different direction from the one established by your club. Without a doubt this superb Dublin course, as far as cleanliness and strictness of its design is concerned, can appear so classic it could be too austere. For true golf connoisseurs, however, this makes the course all the more appealing, truly worthy of being ranked among the best links in the world. The course has the right amount of obstacles, and they are all perfectly placed, ready to swallow the ball with sand traps. Infamous bunkers and impenetrable roughs that surround the fairways are more than enough to frustrate even the best players. Completing the picture are enormous greens, hard to figure out and usually fast, dourly defended by unforgivable bunkers that turn any par into a hopeless dream.

The clubhouse was recently completely refurbished in a classic style at a cost of about five million euros. The classic style fits well with the sobriety of this magnificent championship course, which every golf enthusiast should test themselves against at least once in their life.

84-85 This aerial photograph shows most of the two courses, the Old, whose first holes were opened in 1893, and the Cashen, designed almost 100 years later by Robert Trent Jones.

84 bottom left The 1st hole requires audacity and two straight, long, low shots, in order to avoid the dunes and the wind.

84 bottom right The 8th hole, a very scary par 3 of 154 yards (141 m) from the championship

tees with four bunkers defending the green.

85 The course on the Shannon estuary is so natural that it seems to have never been touched by man. Even Tom Watson's intervention in 1995 did not alter its essence.

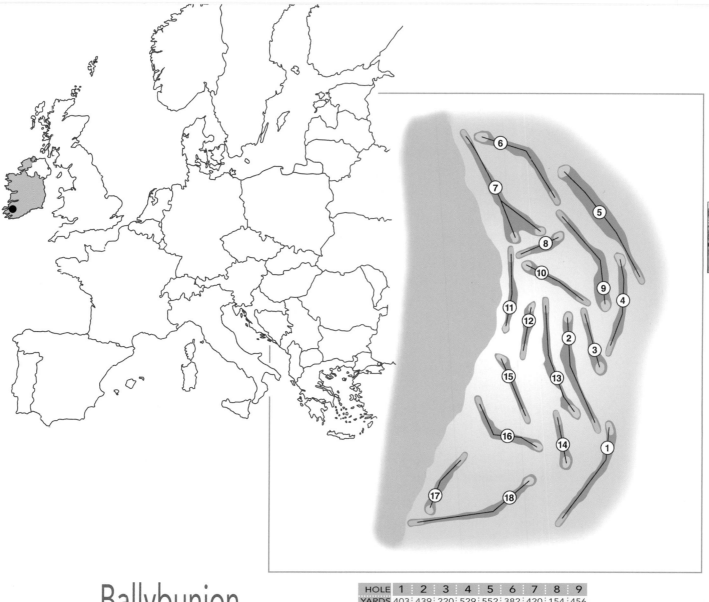

Ballybunion

IRELAND

HOLE	1	2	3	4	5	6	7	8	9
YARDS	403	439	220	529	552	382	420	154	456
PAR	4	4	3	5	5	4	4	3	4

HOLE	10	11	12	13	14	15	16	17	18		TOT
YARDS	361	451	200	486	135	212	499	376	379		6654
PAR	4	4	3	5	3	3	5	4	4		71

In August 1893, two local daily papers reported the same news: the opening of the 12-hole course of the Ballyburion Golf Club, "with every green on a dune." Four years later another daily paper, the *Irish Times*, would criticize the course, comparing it to "a wild rabbit field... where golfers must arm themselves with much patience and an infinite supply of balls." With more detractors than enthusiasts, the club died a financial death in 1898. However, in 1906 it rose again with nine holes designed by Lionel Hewson, who for many years was the editor of *Irish Golf*. From then on Ballybunion's reputation began to spread, attracting golfers from all over the country until the number of holes had to be doubled to 18 in 1927. The links achieved national fame in 1932 when it was chosen to host the Irish Ladies Championship. Five years later, in preparation for a male amateur tournament, the famous golf-course architect Tom Simpson was called in to revise and correct the course. Simpson was so enthusiastic with what he saw that he recommended only two important changes, moving holes 7 and 13, and some minor adjustments, such as the addition of a mid-fairway bunker on what today is the 1st hole. This very bunker, which is known as Mrs. Simpson, has triggered a host of opposing opinions and is still to this day the center of many heated arguments.

Another important date for Ballybunion is 1971, the year in which more land was purchased in order to build a second course, the Cashen, which was created by Robert Trent Jones.

The old clubhouse was abandoned and a new one was built in between the two courses. On the occasion of the club's centennial, in 1993, the brave decision was taken to tear down this clubhouse and build one that would launch Ballybunion into the 21st century. Finally, in 1995 Tom Watson, who became a regular of the Old Course since he played it for the first time in 1981, gave the course one last touch, adapting it to the new century without altering its essence. All this work has been so well done that it almost seems that man never set hand on this links on the Shannon estuary, on the Atlantic coast of Ireland. It is a course with harsh characteristics and a wild look, lacking trees but with the largest dunes in the British Isles, popping up all over the place and covered in long tufts of grass.

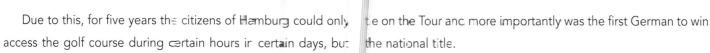

90 The disruption of the Second World War did reach the Hamburger Golf Club. The driving range and five fairways were converted to agricultural use.

When in 1945 the club was seized by the Allies, the course was seriously damaged and the fairways were covered with shell fragments and craters left by bombs.

Due to this, for five years the citizens of Hamburg could only access the golf course during certain hours in certain days, but eventually the course was fully reopened in 1950.

The following period of prosperity meant a steady increase in the number of members, and their fees enabled the club to make so many improvements that it became an internationally renowned championship course. Although some 20 or so golf clubs have popped up around the city, the Hamburger Golf – as it is still called today – remains the most revered. It was the venue for the 1981 German Open, where a 24-year old Bernhard Langer, who had been a pro for seven years, won his second ti-

te on the Tour and more importantly was the first German to win the national title.

After having hosted the Open eight times, the course is now considered too short (6382 yards/5836 m, par 71) for the modern game, but it continues to offer players a good challenge, with its holes branching out in all directions, large, well-kept greens, fairways lined with trees and bushes, well-placed bunkers, and numerous slopes. The soil rests on a sandy base, which ensures proper drainage and the possibility to play the course during rainy months. The hardest hole is the 2nd, a par 5 of 549 yards (502 m), straight and narrow; its greatest obstacle is the surrounding trees.

Hamburger Falkenstein

90-91 and 91 bottom The post-war economic boom gradually increased the number of members, whose fees allowed for so many improvements that it became an internationally renowned championship course. It was the venue for the 1981 German Open, where a 24-year old Bernhard Langer, a seven-year pro, won his second title on the Tour and, more importantly, was the first German to win the national title.

Valderrama

106 top The 6th hole, nicknamed El Vallejo, is a par 3 of 164 yards (149 m) and its tee is raised 26 ft (8 m) above the green.

106 bottom The number and size of the bunkers, the water hazards, and the difficult-to-read greens constantly keep players thinking.

Named *Muy Dificil*, the 16th is "one of the toughest par 4s I've ever faced," said Ronan Rafferty after winning the 1989 Volvo Masters. For years the 17th was a hell of a par 5 and then, after some hard thinking, the management decided to add a lake in front of the green. Today, the 536 yard (490 m) long hole is the most talked about. It requires precision and a good eye for distance, especially on the second shot when preparing for the third, which must cross the water. Should I fly over it first to lower the score or should I play it safe? Miguel Angel Jiménez went for the challenge at the 1995 Volvo Masters and made the first albatross of his life – and the first of the course. In the 2000 World Golf Championships, the lake swallowed the golf balls of many players who closed with a bogey or double-bogey, while others flew over it for an easy birdie. Lastly, the 18th is a complicated par 4 with a left dogleg. Those who dare can decide to cut through it by flying over the trees and will be rewarded by the best approach to this well-protected green.

Besides the artificial hazards, nature also plays a decisive role with the two prevailing winds requiring a great variety of shots on a course which already demands a whole host of them. The countless trees, the bunkers, the water hazards, and the difficult to read greens keep players constantly on the edge. In short, it is best not to think about your handicap and enjoy a course that is so well-kept that you can see the green-keepers constantly bent over the fairway, ripping out weeds with their hands. In fact, besides Loch Lomond, Valderrama is the only European course to be certified a Cooperative Sanctuary by Audubon, an American company whose mission it is to preserve natural ecosystems

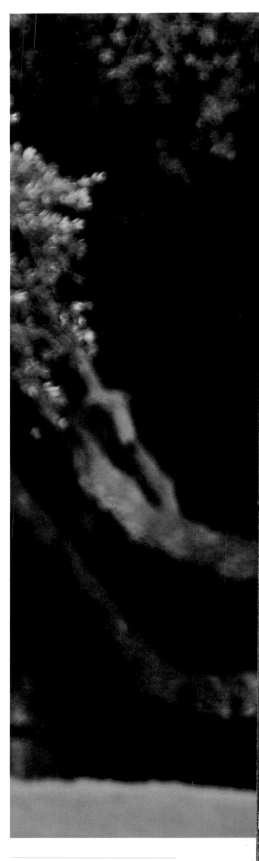

106-107 Valderrama was the venue for the Volvo Masters from 1988 to 1996 and, in 1997, for the 32nd Ryder Cup, the only European club to host it outside of the U.S.A. and Britain. Among the pros that have walked its fairways is the Scottish champ Colin Montgomery.

107 bottom The first modification decided by the new owner and Robert Trent Jones was the inversion of the first and the second nine. The adjustments to the final four holes have made them better than their old counterparts.

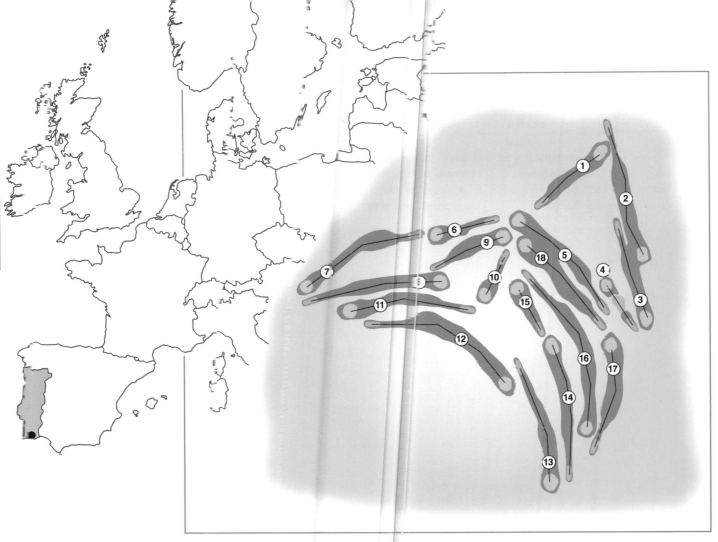

Vilamoura

PORTUGAL

HOLE	1	2	3	4	5	6	7	8	9
YARDS	339	476	354	178	530	232	430	458	399
PAR	4	5	4	3	5	3	4	4	4

HOLE	10	11	12	13	14	15	16	17	18
YARDS	167	427	535	381	481	164	562	386	452
PAR	3	4	5	4	5	3	5	4	4

TOT
6949
73

The Algarve is one Europe's golf paradises. As happened on Spain's Costa del Sol, the building of golf courses was at the center of the development plan for the region. Along slightly more than 62 miles (100 km) of coast facing the Atlantic there are about 30 courses available to the tourists who flock to the Algarve every year, via Lisbon or, even better, Faro, the region's capital. Faro and its international airport are more or less at the center of this stretch of coast, and are therefore capable of efficiently serving all the courses of this the southernmost region of Portugal.

The area's pride is Vilamoura, which has a number of excellent courses. Its location is slightly inland from the nearby beaches, and about 20 minutes by car from Faro's airport. The "venerable splendor" of the Old Course at Vilamoura, one of the first courses built in the Algarve, has remained a symbol for all those who are passionate about golf in Portugal. But the more recent Victoria course has been equally successful and even rivals its prestigious companion. There is a fascinating and friendly duel between these two great courses.

It was in 1969 when Vilamoura (subsequently renamed the Old Course) opened its doors. A creation of Frank Pennink, a prolific designer of courses in Portugal, the Old Course closely followed the design of the two courses at Vale do Lobo (the Ocean and the Royal Golf Course), which had initiated in 1968 the rapid development of golf in Portugal. Today, the Old Course is in the middle of a major Portuguese resort created for golfers and which includes another four courses – Laguna, Millennium, Pinhal, and the already mentioned Victoria – providing a total of 90 holes. Surrounding the more traditional course are residential buildings constructed between 1973 and 2005, and a continual modernization program is planned by the Oceânico Group, who owns the entire resort. The management was given to Troon Golf.

Frank Pennink's design of the Old Course maintained all the charm of its magnificent natural environment and rich vegetation. In certain areas, the design is reminiscent of prestigious British courses, with the added advantage of a very pleasant climate during most of the year. Often described as the "Grande Dame" of the Algarve courses, the Old Course's magnificent umbrella pines are a player's most unyielding adversaries. The 18 holes measure 6949 yards (6354 m), with the unusual par of 73 due to the three par 5s on the back nine. Length is therefore not the most testing characteristic of Pennink's course. There are many other hazards that make it a stimulating challenge, such as the fairly narrow fairways, the tough greens, the well-placed bunkers and the vegetation. In contrast, water hazards are the major kind of hazard encountered at Victoria, which was designed by the great Arnold Palmer.

110-111 The historic course of Vilamoura (later renamed Old Course) opened to enthusiasts in 1969. It was designed by Frank Pennink then revised in 1996 by Martin Hawtree to keep pace with the constant development of golf equipment.

111 bottom The Old Course is part of the largest Portuguese golf resort, which includes five courses for a total of 90 holes. The other courses are Laguna, Millennium, Pinhal, and Victoria, while the second jewel, Vilamoura, bears the signature of Arnold Palmer.

112-113 Luke Donald attempting to exit the bunker on the 14th hole of the Victoria course at Vilamoura, during one of the prestigious matches hosted by the Portuguese resort, the 2005 World Golf Championship.

112 bottom Luke Donald and David Howell observe the direction of the shot towards the 13th hole of the Victoria at Vilamoura.

Vilamoura

113 Important tournaments have made the most beautiful Algarve courses famous in only a few years. The Old Course at Vilamoura is particularly outstanding with its magnificent setting, the rich vegetation, and its superb design, which in certain parts is reminiscent of the most prestigious British parkland courses.

In order to modernize it and keep it up to date, the Old Course was closed in 1996 and Martin Hawtree was called in to manage the restructuring. As they could not significantly increase the course's length, which was nonetheless adjusted a little compared to the original design, they narrowed down the fairways and this had the effect of making the looming presence of the pines ever larger and more majestic. The result of the restructuring was superlative and rejuvenated this classy international course.

114-115 This aerial view highlights the incomparable position of the Crans-sur-Sierre club, a veritable balcony in the Valais Alps facing south.

114 bottom The European Masters has a permanent venue at the gorgeous Crans-sur-Sierre course, which thanks to the most important Swiss competition is by far the most famous Swiss golf course in the world. The arrival at the 18th hole is always an emotional one, with the audience densely crowded around the green.

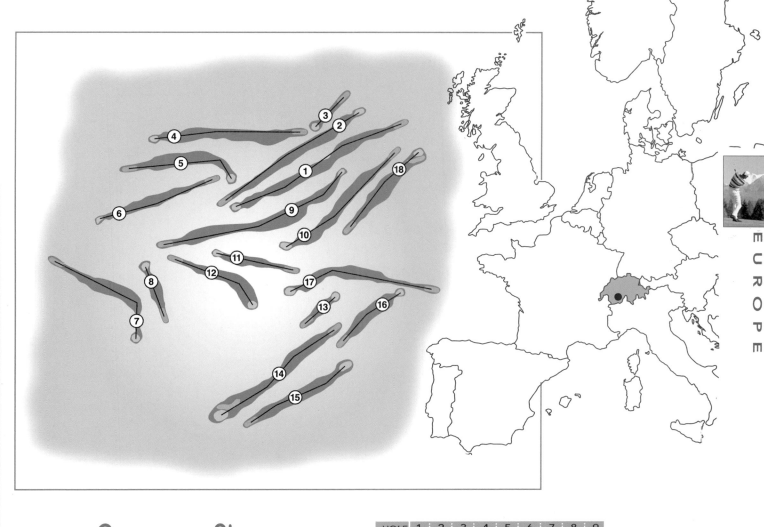

Crans-sur-Sierre

SWITZERLAND

HOLE	1	2	3	4	5	6	7	8	9
YARDS	540	437	191	503	339	324	331	175	629
PAR	5	4	3	4	4	4	4	3	5

HOLE	10	11	12	13	14	15	16	17	18		TOT
YARDS	405	205	410	199	595	516	347	386	402		6934
PAR	4	3	4	3	5	5	4	4	4		72

As far as beauty is concerned this course, the most famous and popular course in Switzerland, has few rivals. Superbly located on a plateau facing the Alps, the Golf Club Crans-sur-Sierre is the permanent venue for the Swiss Open, a tournament that takes place throughout the courses of the Confederation. First held in 1923, the Swiss Open maintained this simple denomination until 1982. The following year, it earned the name "European Masters," which, in 1992, became exclusive to Crans. The European Masters, which is held in early September, is normally accompanied by the name of a sponsor (first Ebel, then Canon and, more recently, Omega).

More or less halfway between Briga and Martigny, in the deep valley formed by the initial course of the Rodano, Sierre is one of the main townships of the Valais Canton. Just 9 miles (15 km) away and at 4900 ft (1500 m) are the ski resorts of Crans and its twin Montana, where important winter sports competitions are held, including the 1987 alpine skiing world championship. However, during the spring and summer months Crans-Montana is known for its golf club. Founded in 1906, the Golf Club de Crans-sur-Sierre attracts thousands of golf enthusiasts not only from all over Switzerland but also from nearby countries, in particular Italy. It is open six months a year, from early May to late October.

The fame of the Valaisian club is due mostly to the Swiss Open, but an equally important attraction is its extraordinary position. The location on the plateau that dominates the val-

ley is unique, with in the distance the highest peaks of the Alps, from Cervino to Mont Blanc. The amazing 360-degree panorama made Greg Norman say that Crans-sur Sierre is "by far the world's most spectacular mountain course." The club does not just rely on its scenery for its fame and the club's management, led by Gaston Barras, work endlessly to improve and expand what the club has to offer. Today, along with the main course, Crans has a nine-hole course of over

115 Severiano Ballesteros was, at 20, the youngest winner of the European Masters held at Crans-sur-Sierre, on the course that today bears his name. The Swiss Open has been here since 1939, though the Second World War meant that it was not held again until 1948, and Crans is now the permanent venue.

Crans-sur-Sierre

2952 yards (2700 m) designed by Jack Nicklaus, two short pitch and putt courses, and a few beginner courses (Noas and Super Crans).

Crans is a classic, well-balanced 18-hole championship course, which was substantially redesigned by Severiano Ballesteros to adapt it to the ever-improving performances of the modern champions of golf. The course today bears the name of the great Spanish champion (who also was the youngest winner of the European Masters, at only 20 years old, in 1977) and was extended to 6934 yards (6340 m), a decent distance if it were not for the fact that in the mountain's rarefied air the balls fly longer. This partly explains the two scores of 60 that, before the Ballesteros revision, were the

course's record, established by the Italian Baldovino Dassù and Britain's Jamie Spence. If played from the beginners' tees, the course is not too hard and will not challenge medium-level players too much. Hazards are quite visible and the difficulties consist mainly in the terrain's irregularity and the trees, which sometimes need to be coped with during a game. There are only two (quite tricky) water hazards near the greens of the 14th and the 18th. The most beautiful hole of the "Severiano Ballesteros" is without a doubt the 7th, a short par 4 of 331 yards (303 m) that the Tour champions easily cut by aiming at the green with their first shot. The view from this hole is truly breathtaking, looking out over most of the Rodano valley: unforgettable.

116 and 116-117 The remarkable critical and popular success of the European Masters at Crans-sur-Sierre is also due to the presence of important sponsors, which have enabled it to maintain its international status. It is not a surprise that recent Masters have featured such names as Garcia, Els, Rocca, Montgomerie, Ballesteros, Olázabal, Westwood, Woosnam, and Faldo.

117 bottom Over the years the course has been extended and made more challenging, to "protect" it from the technological developments of the modern game. It now has a length of 6934 yards (6340 m).

118-119 and 119 Crans-sur-Sierre's
incredible location in the Alps
provides incomparable views from
the Severiano Ballesteros Course,
which takes its name from the
legendary Spanish champion who

a few years ago supervised its
complete revision. The most
spectacular hole is by far the 7th,
a short par 4 of 331 yards (303 m),
considered among the world's
most beautiful mountain holes.

Crans-sur-Sierre

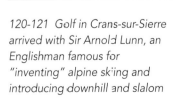

120-121 Golf in Crans-sur-Sierre arrived with Sir Arnold Lunn, an Englishman famous for "inventing" alpine skiing and introducing downhill and slalom skiiung to the Winter Olympics. Lunn decided to build an 18-hole course in 1905. Construction began the following year and ended in 1908.

126-127 and 126 bottom
The modern clubhouse at
Castelconturbia dominates the
convergence of the three courses
(Blue, Yellow, and Red). The
courses were designed by the
great American architect Robert
Trent Jones.

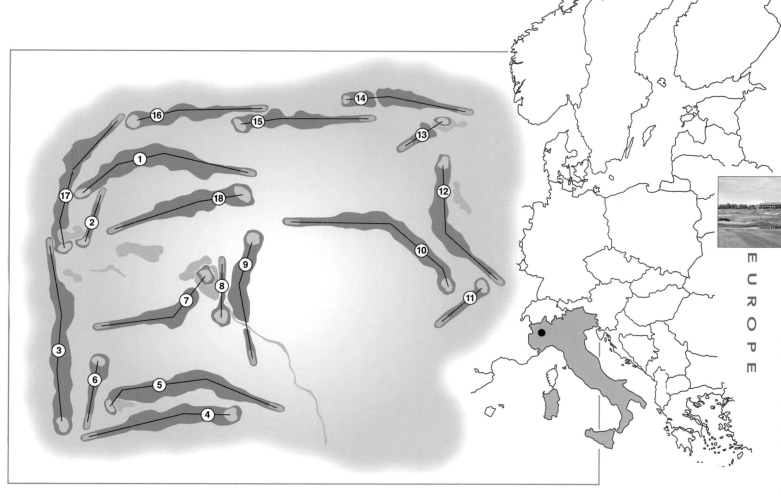

Castelconturbia

ITALY

HOLE	1	2	3	4	5	6	7	8	9
YARDS	534	168	550	441	544	190	381	192	374
PAR	5	3	5	4	5	3	4	3	4

HOLE	10	11	12	13	14	15	16	17	18		TOT
YARDS	562	162	445	151	374	405	409	521	411		6814
PAR	5	3	4	3	4	4	4	5	4		72

The spectacle that greets you from the terrace of the clubhouse of Castelconturbia is unforgettable. To admire the course on a beautiful late spring or autumn evening is truly one of the most beautiful sights in golf. Designed by the great Robert Trent Jones, the 27 holes of this magnificent Italian club end with three different upward slopes towards the clubhouse, which dominates them from above with its long, ocher-yellow outline. Inside the clubhouse there are huge halls, with every type of service and amenity, and a pleasant lodge with about 20 rooms. A few miles from Lake Maggiore and less than an hour from Milan by car, the Golf Castelconturbia Club is considered by many to be the best in Italy and among the best in Europe. The three nine-hole courses (Yellow Pine Course, Blue Chestnut Course, and the Red Oak Tree Course) are technical and spectacular, with a respectable level of difficulty – the course record is a score of 66, shot by José Maria Olazábal and Costantino Rocca.

Opened in 1986, the club actually has a complex history. In 1898 its ancestor, the Couturbier Golf Club, was the only course in Piedmont, as recorded by certain books of the day. The founder was Count Gaspar Voli, who was famous for his many trips to Scotland, where he had the chance to familiarize with and learn golf.

His passion for the game had grown to the point where he involved his neighbor, Count Avogadro di Colombiano, and convinced him to build nine holes on his estate. A meeting place for the members of the House of Savoy, who would gather here for fox hunts, the course was a par 36 of 2000 yards (1828 m). With varying fortunes, the course was operative until around 1963. No longer open to the public and strictly private, it was eventually abandoned and remained so for a couple of decades.

However, the magnificent, rich land of forests and gentle hills, dominated by the huge silhouette of the Monte Rosa massif, felt as though it was purposely made for golf. It was no surprise, therefore, that in 1984 the club was reestablished and one after the other all three courses were reopened. The great British-born, American architect Robert Trent Jones was hired to redesign over one square kilometer of terrain. The result was superb and Trent Jones considered Castelconturbia to be one of his finest works.

He refurbished and widened the area where the old nine holes used to be, and worked with great enthusiasm in this countryside with its venerable trees, delightful streams, and picturesque small lakes, all perfect natural obstacles for a golf course.

The championship course, which incorporates holes of the Yellow and Blue courses, has hosted many important events, among them the 1991 and 1998 Italian Opens, which were considered to be among the best in the history of the competition. Nestled in a magnificent forest, the championship course is over 6800 yards (6200 m) and is a true test of even the greatest players. The Red Course, however, is by no means inferior to the others and it impeccably completes the club's range.

Castelconturbia

128 The greens at Castelconturbia are very undulating and are difficult to read, typical of a Trent Jones design. They are among the most challenging of Italy's golf courses.

128-129 The beautiful 7th hole of the Yellow Course at Castelconturbia is considered the signature hole. The island green frames the last holes of three courses and the clubhouse, which, on clear days is crowned by the Monte Rosa massif in the background.

As with all the best Robert Trent Jones designs, the greens are extremely challenging as they are complex with tricky slopes, and players always run the risk of taking more than the regular two putts. Then there are bunkers, wide, well placed, and liberally scattered all over the three courses. The most beautiful hole is probably the 7th on the Yellow Course, which is a true masterpiece that is often considered one of the best in the world by the most prestigious golf magazines. It is a long par 4 between two high rows of trees, with an abrupt left dogleg, while the island green frames the last holes of three courses and the clubhouse, which, on clear days is crowned by the Monte Rosa massif – a picture postcard scene.

129 bottom Castelconturbia's course features some water hazards that really put players with high handicaps to the test, such as the one in front of the green of the 8th (17th hole) on the Blue, a nice par 5 of 521 yards (476 m).

Le Méridien Moscow

132 The design of the Moscow was completed by Robert Trent Jones Jr., who thought of it as a classic parkland where the trees (most of them tall beeches) play a discreet part in the game.

The prettiest aspect of the course is definitely its relationship with the forest and the surrounding countryside. In fact the entire estate covers 300 acres (120 hectares), where golf can go wild with these ample spaces, and the level of maintenance is excellent, on a par with the best European courses. Even though the design of the course is typically American, the massive presence of numerous birches, pines, and larches, and the many ponds and lakes scattered throughout the area, leaves no doubt that we are in the heart of Russia. From a technical point of view, the presence of several starting tees allows the Moscow Country Club course to be tackled by players of all abilities and is challenging enough to test the ability of even the very best golfers.

133 bottom The estate of the Moscow Country Club covers 300 acres (120 hectares) of land, surrounded by a thick forest. The presence of many small bodies of water allowed Trent Jones Jr. to incorporate these natural hazards into at least eight holes, making the course more varied and interesting.

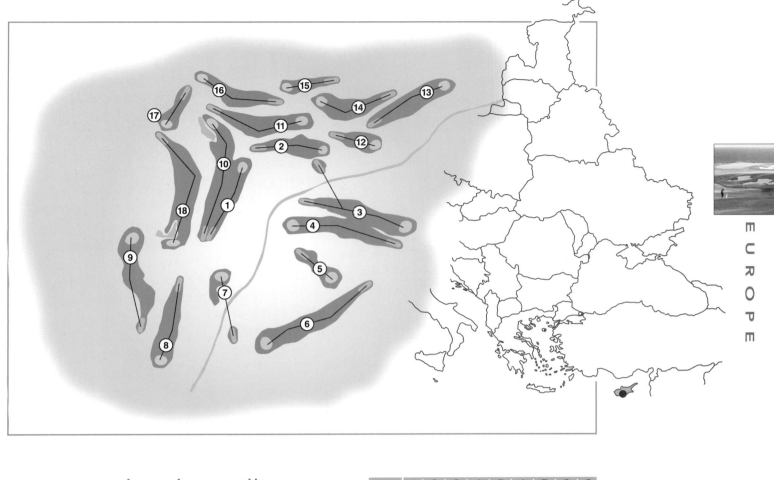

Aphrodite Hills

CYPRUS

HOLE	1	2	3	4	5	6	7	8	9
YARDS	394	367	573	405	154	500	210	323	362
PAR	4	4	4/5	4	3	5	3	4	4

HOLE	10	11	12	13	14	15	16	17	18		TOT
YARDS	508	390	188	377	331	209	399	165	484		6299
PAR	5	4	3	4	4	3	4	3	5		70/71

Myth has it that the Greek goddess of beauty and love, Aphrodite (Venus for the Romans), was born out of the sea foam off the southern coast of Cyprus, more precisely, not too far from present-day Paphos, where the Petra tou Romiou ("Rock of the Greek") emerges from the sea. A beautiful corner of the Mediterranean. Just a brief drive from the legendary beach is a short road that climbs up into the low, inland hills towards the Aphrodite Hills golf club, which takes its name from the goddess. Welcoming golfers is a modern and sophisticated clubhouse, which is located in the easternmost corner of the course and has a terrace that dominates the wide and undulating 18th hole. Across the road is the equally luxurious five-star Intercontinental hotel, which is the center of the whole Aphrodite Hills resort, located in the hills that surround the golf course.

The course was designed by the American architect Cabell B. Robinson, long-time manager of Robert Trent Jones' European office, and much of its charm is due to the harsh, bare countryside. The contrast with the velvety fairways and greens could not be more impressively stark. Also fascinating is the complex interplay of different levels on which the holes have been placed, which line and cross the deep gorges. A total of 10 million euros was spent on creating the course. This huge cost was largely required because of the difficulty of creating a course in these harsh conditions and with such poor-quality soil.

The large plateaus on which the course is distributed in-

clude two important water hazards (on the par 5 10th and 18th holes), which balance the wide areas dominated by olive trees and carobs. The rest of the vegetation includes typically Mediterranean bushes, which are skillfully placed on all the holes. Despite being quite short (about 6290 yards/5750 m from the men's tee and with a par of 71), what is amazing about Aphrodite Hills is its ability to constantly appear different each time it is played.

134-135 The Aphrodite Hills course, Cyprus, sprawls out over a rocky plateau divided by deep gorges, in a beautiful setting, abundant with typical Mediterranean flora. In the photo one can see the 7th hole.

134 bottom and 135 The most recent and most spectacular course in Cyprus is the gorgeous Aphrodite Hills, which takes its name from the goddess of beauty, who, as legend has it, was born from the sea at a spot only a few hundred yards from the resort.

136 and 136-137 Aphrodite Hills Golf was designed in the early years of the 21st century by Canadian architect Cabell B. Robinson. It was then joined by one of the island's most beautiful resorts, the luxurious Intercontinental Aphrodite Hills, providing every type of service and comfort.

Aphrodite Hills

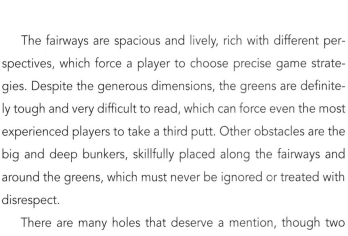

137 From the covered pool to the large spa with massage and treatment areas, from the suites to the conference halls, at the Intercontinental Aphrodite Hills everything was designed to provide a high-class vacation or to relax after 18 holes on the magnificent golf course. The clubhouse is located exactly in front of hotel entrance.

The fairways are spacious and lively, rich with different perspectives, which force a player to choose precise game strategies. Despite the generous dimensions, the greens are definitely tough and very difficult to read, which can force even the most experienced players to take a third putt. Other obstacles are the big and deep bunkers, skillfully placed along the fairways and around the greens, which must never be ignored or treated with disrespect.

There are many holes that deserve a mention, though two holes in particular rise above the others. The first is the 7th, one of the world's prettiest par 3s, which is reached by a dizzying downhill path where you better keep your foot on the brake pedal of your cart (which are obligatory on this course) to avoid surprises. The long, thin tee is situated on a rock, which supports it along the whole right side. In front, on the other side of the canyon, you can see the welcoming green, which can be approached from distances between 125 and 207 yards (115 and 190 m) for men, while women can even avoid the whole obstacle by playing on the other side of the precipice. If the shot is successful, you can ride the cart down into the heart of the canyon then back up the other side to the green, which is surrounded by bunkers and ancient olive trees. The view from the next hole, the 8th, a short downhill par 4, looks out towards the expanse of the Mediterranean. The well-protected green seems literally poised above the sea, and provides an intensely gorgeous view. Another memorable hole is the 3rd, the hardest of the course if played from the men's back tee, with a first shot that must cover 165 yards (150 m) over a deep canyon and onto a higher level. In this case the hole, which is usually a nice par 4, turns into a tough par 5, reserved for players with a cool head and a long solid drive. The course closes with the beautiful 18th, which is a wide par 5 that becomes rather demanding due to the broad water hazard jutting out to the right of the fairway and in front of the green. A truly impressive finish.

138 Two news of the Aphrodite Hills green and, bottom, the 8th hole, is a slightly downhill par 4, which offers a gorgeous view of the Mediterranean. Olive and carob trees are the most common plants along this course, which unfolds over the rocky hills of the southern part of Cyprus, the third largest island of the Mediterranean (after Sicily and Sardinia).

139 The downslope towards the tee of the 7th hole is the signature hole of Aphrodite Hills Golf. It is a par 3 of incredible impact, where players need to make the ball fly over the deep canyon before landing on the green. An extremely long tee allows players to vary the distance of the shot from a simple pitch to a more demanding long iron.

Aphrodite Hills

AFRICA

As far as golf is concerned, Africa is a continent that has yet to be discovered. Although the continent's golf history began about one hundred years ago, its development still remains relatively limited. The only exception is South Africa, where golf became popular in the late 19th century. This southernmost country of the continent is where golf was first played in Africa. The date is quite precise, it was 14th November 1885 when Sir Henry Torrens was elected head of the Cape Golf Club, a club very close to beautiful Cape Town. A few years later, King George V allowed the South African club to add "Royal" to its name, a privilege granted to only the most prestigious establishments. The same thing happened to the Nairobi Club, established in 1906, which once again became "Royal" thanks to the same king. The magnificent Dar Es Salam in Rabat was also titled royal, because it was King Hassan II of Morocco's favorite club. Three similar stories in three very different places, so far from one another, yet linked by the history of golf in Africa.

There are more than 350 courses and 120,000 golfers in the Republic of South Africa, which makes it by far the most developed golfing nation in Africa. Along its marvelous ocean coasts, in the precious vineyard regions, and in its grasslands, spectacular courses were created as exclusive refuges reserved for the Europeans only. In recent times, fortunately, the country has thrown off apartheid and now resorts and facilities for all are being constructed. Tourism has become a major in-

dustry and South Africa is especially appealing to tourists from the northern hemisphere who seek to escape their winters. The result is an ever-increasing number of Europeans heading south to enjoy the marvelous weather and stunning countryside of this distant country. One of the great attractions is, of course, the country's golf courses, which are nobly represented by such great South African players as Gary Player, Ernie Els, and Retief Goosen.

The rest of Africa has very few courses in comparison (approximately 150), though there are several real gems, such as the already mentioned Dar Es Salam just outside Rabat. After South Africa, Morocco is the next force in African golf. It has many large-scale tourism projects being developed on its Mediterranean and Atlantic coasts that always include golf as an essential component. Similar developments are appearing in Tunisia and Egypt, thanks to new agronomic technology and grass that requires little water. Aided by low-cost flights, the Mediterranean regions are keen on attracting golfers from northern European countries, who are only two or three hours away, by creating excellent new courses. While elsewhere, Kenya, Namibia, and Nigeria also have significant golf facilities. Other African countries belonging to the International Golf Federation are Côte d'Ivoire, Gabon, and Swaziland.

From one end of the continent to the other there are little more than 500 courses, less than those available in Germany alone. After all, in Africa, golf cannot be considered a top priority. There are more important things to think about.

---

140 left The Royal Dar Es Salam, Rabat, Morocco.

140 right The Pezula Golf Club is the best in South Africa.

141 A white coral beach 1 mile (2 km) long and 37 acres (15

hectares) of gardens are a perfect frame for Belle Mare.

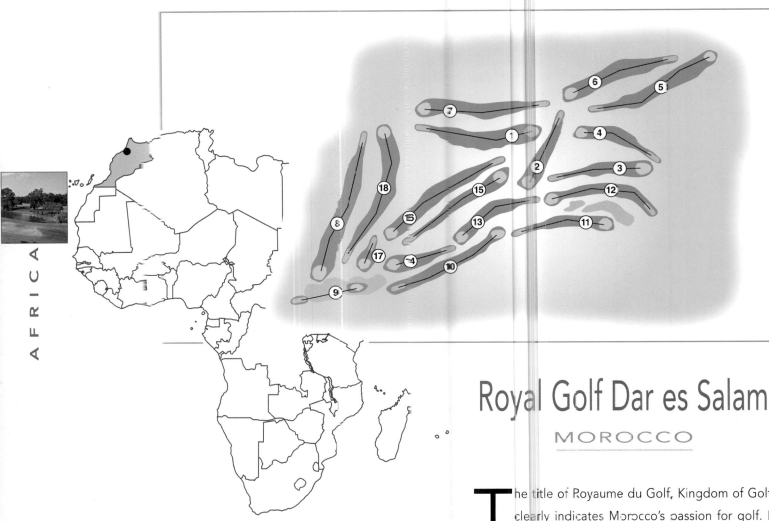

HOLE	1	2	3	4	5	6	7	8	9
YARDS	400	232	42	404	565	440	420	582	188
PAR	4	3	4	4	5	4	4	5	3

HOLE	10	11	12	13	14	15	16	17	18		TOT
YARDS	481	467	52e	384	206	390	424	225	552		7329
PAR	5	4	5	4	3	4	4	3	5		73

Royal Golf Dar es Salam

MOROCCO

The title of Royaume du Golf, Kingdom of Golf, clearly indicates Morocco's passion for golf. It is home to one of the oldest courses in Africa. The recent kings of Morocco never hid their passion for the game and they created several interesting courses. The best of these were granted the "Royal" title, including Fès, Meknès, Agadir, and Marrakech. The absolute "king" is the Royal Golf Dar Es Salam, near Rabat, which was the favorite golf course of King Hassan II, who died in 1999 at the age of 70. Hassan II was a member of the Alaouita dynasty, which has reigned over Morocco since 1666. He was a true golf enthusiast and helped to develop golf in his North African country. The game first arrived in the 1920s, introduced by a few English players. His private teachers were Claude Harmon and his son Butch, both famous American pros and often considered the best golf teachers in the world.

The most important sports event of the year is dedicated to Hassan II and takes place at the beautiful Royal Golf Dar Es Salam. The Hassan II Trophy was inaugurated in 1971 and the list of its winners includes international stars such as Billy Casper, Lee Trevino, Vijay Singh, Payne Stewart, Colin Montgomerie, Sam Torrance, and Padraig Harrington. A fairly high-class venue, often ranked among the best golf courses in the world, the Royal Golf Dar Es Salam is the stuff of legend in Morocco. It owes its fame to the creative genius of Robert Trent Jones, who designed it in 1971. In that same year, Jones and Claude Harmon, who were hired to supervise the works, almost lost their lives during the first of the government coups that were a feature of the reign of Hassan II, who nonetheless remained on the throne for 38 years.

The Dar Es Salam is about 6 miles (10 km) from Rabat and consists of 45 holes, divided into three courses, Red, Blue, and Green. The hardest one is definitely the Red, which is the venue for all the important competitions.

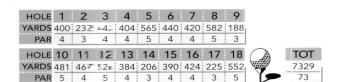

142 The "royal" club of Rabat is definitely the most famous in Morocco. It is consists of 45 holes divided into two 18-hole courses, the Red and the Blue, and the nine-hole Green.

142-143 and 143 bottom Robert Trent Jones is the architect that designed the very beautiful Red course upon the request of King Hassan II, a great golf enthusiast. Jones completed the job in 1971.

146-147 The first task carried out by the founder of Pezula, Keith Stewart, was to clear 1000 acres (400 hectares) of land in order to restore the original brush, which now makes up the rough.

146 bottom Modern, bright, and quite large, the clubhouse reflects the immense area, 627 acres (254 hectares), of the course – so large that the use of a cart is obligatory.

147 After having acquired 1512 acres (612 hectares) of land, Keith Stewart then bought the nearby Sparrebosch Golf Club, which he renamed and renovated its clubhouse.

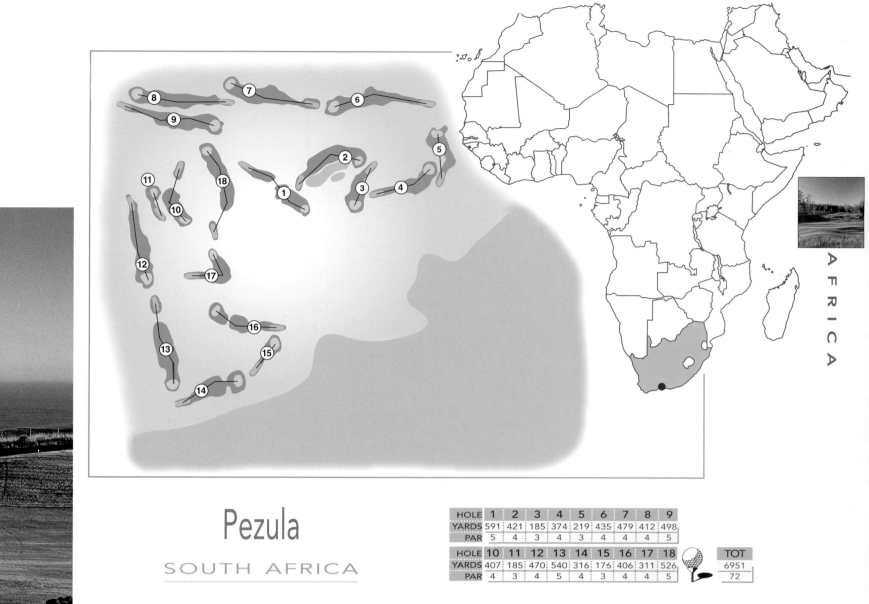

Pezula

SOUTH AFRICA

HOLE	1	2	3	4	5	6	7	8	9
YARDS	591	421	185	374	219	435	479	412	498
PAR	5	4	3	4	3	4	4	4	5

HOLE	10	11	12	13	14	15	16	17	18		TOT
YARDS	407	185	470	540	316	176	406	311	526		6951
PAR	4	3	4	5	4	3	4	4	5		72

Keith Stewart had a dream to create a world-class luxury resort in one of the most beautiful areas of the world in South Africa. Stewart was born in Great Britain, raised in Zimbabwe, and became rich in the United States. In the 1990s, when he returned to Africa he looked for a site to realize his dream. In 2000, he found an area of 1512 acres (612 hectares) on the Garden Route, near the city of George, bordered by the craggy reefs of the Southern Cape. He named it Pezula, which means "up there with the gods," and his first objective was to restore the land to its natural state after 100 years of exploitation as a plantation. He began by clearing 1000 acres (400 hectares) of vegetation and brushwood in order to restore the original scrub and obtained the permission to urbanize a small part of it (only 15 percent) with low-density residential buildings. He then acquired the adjacent Sparrebosch Golf Club, renamed it, refurbished the clubhouse, and ultimately created a five-star hotel. Thus was created the Pezula Golf Club, high up on the massive cape on the African coast and at the entrance of the Knysna lagoon.

Carved out of the terrain by David Dale and Donald Fream on an ever-changing stretch of coast, it is one of the world's most spectacular courses. According to the same architects, the course is reminiscent of Gleneagles in Scotland. The Scottish feel extends to the eyebrow bunkers and the intensity of the wind, one of the constant hazards. Pezula is a course that puts every type of shot on the menu and therefore offers a challenging golf experience, rewarding and complete, for players of all levels, thanks also to the five tee options that lengthen the course from 5140 to about 7000 yards (4700 to 6400 m). Every hole offers a different challenge and a new treat for the eyes: every hole has a view of the Indian Ocean and from some you can see the lagoon. It is an undulating expanse – almost like a rollercoaster – as well as immense (627 acres/254 hectares) which means that holes are often very far from one another, separated by large, fragrant scrubs of fynbos (the native shrubs typical of this short stretch of coast) and difficult to cover on foot, so much so that you need approximately five hours to play it, including a small break halfway through. The golf carts, fully equipped with GPS, are mandatory, but, as helpful as they can be, they do not always provide the information that would be helpful in blind blows on the uphill and downhill slopes of this terrain: a caddie would be much more helpful, especially for first-time players of this course.

After an unusual initial par 5 (the hardest hole of the course), which immediately erases any doubt about whether this course is

Pezula

a breeze or not, the course moves away from the ocean and includes a few holes along the cliffs facing the city of Knysna. Two of the best are the 2nd (par 4) and 3rd (par 3) holes, but all eyes are on the inward nine, played along the coastal part of the resort, towards the ocean. The most famous of all are the trio of the 13th, 14th, and 15th on the reef. The 14th is the trickiest: a short par 4 of 316 yards (289 m) with the most sensational backdrop. It is probably better to follow a balanced approach rather than to try an aggressive game with a drive, because the green is completely surrounded by bunkers. Therefore, make sure not to go too long or you will end up out of bounds – beyond the cliffs.

148-149 The open, rolling terrain makes the holes quite far apart from each other and it would be a very long and hard course to play on foot. Although every cart is equipped with a GPS system, they cannot provide the kind of information that caddies can with their direct knowledge of the land, so useful in blind shots.

148 bottom "Pezula" means "up there with the gods," and that is how the owner of this resort must have felt when he finally found the land. The resort was built by David Dale and Ronald Fream on an ever-changing coastal tract that allowed the construction of a golf course that has a view of the Indian Ocean and the Knysna lagoon from every hole.

149 top In addition to the rough, the holes are also separated by fynbos brush. According to the same architects, this course is reminiscent of the look of Gleneagles in the Scottish Highlands, in part thanks to the look of the "eyebrow" bunkers.

149 bottom The reflectors are pointed on the second nine, holes near the ocean, but even the first nine include some interesting and challenging holes, featuring a few trees that damp the wind.

150-151 The Resort of Belle Mare Plage has two golf courses, the Links and the Legend, which from 1974 has been the venue for the Mauritius Golf Open, the most important tournament of the Indian Ocean. The Legend, which is situated in an ancient deer reserve, is the work of the South African Hugh Baiocchi.

150 bottom The rooms of the hotel face the sea or the golf course: guests can choose their favorite view.

151 Water and bunkers protect the 17th hole, a par 3, at the Legend. The lakes, often covered in lilies, are an ever-present obstacle at the Legend.

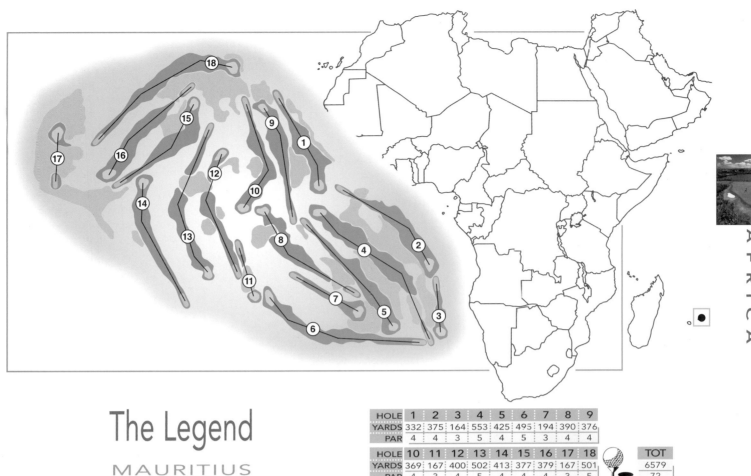

The Legend

MAURITIUS

HOLE	1	2	3	4	5	6	7	8	9
YARDS	332	375	164	553	425	495	194	390	376
PAR	4	4	3	5	4	5	3	4	4

HOLE	10	11	12	13	14	15	16	17	18		TOT
YARDS	369	167	400	502	413	377	379	167	501		6579
PAR	4	3	4	5	4	4	4	3	5		72

I f the climate is what makes Mauritius a perfect vacation destination whatever the season, then the Legend is what makes it a wonderful golf destination. The first of the two courses of the Constance Belle Mare Plage resort opened in January 1994 (the second course, the Links, opened in 2002) and was designed by Hugh Baiocchi, the South African champion. He created the course on 173 acres (70 hectares) of an ancient deer reserve. In some areas the course has been carved out of the bush-covered volcanic rocks, while in other parts it spreads onto the floodplains.

Mauritius is a pearl in the Mascarenes, a group of islands in the Indian Ocean east of Madagascar. This independent republic has English as its official language and is quite distinct from the other famous islands of the area, such as Réunion (125 miles/200 km to the southwest), which speaks French and as an overseas *département* of France is the most distant part of the European Union. With one of the highest per capita income rates in Africa and a stable democracy established in 1968 after the declaration of independence, Mauritius has established a prosperous economy, which has developed away from agriculture into finance and tourism. The tourist sector is by far the most successful part of the island's economy, thanks to its beauty and wonderful tropical climate. As Mark Twain wrote: "You gather the idea that Mauritius was made first, and then heaven; and that heaven was copied after Mauritius."

Golf here is rather new, but it has quickly made up for lost time and there are now several 9- and 18-hole courses that can use the stunning scenery to good effect to offer breathtaking holes. The Mauritius Golf Open, which takes place in December, is the main competitive event and has always been associated with the first course, the Constance Belle Mare Plage. On the Legend, golfers have very few chances to relax before getting to the 18th, unless they are really good at reaching the fairways. If they are not, then in order to recover lost balls one would have to struggle into the jungle or dive into the sea, which Baiocchi has made a constant hazard. Nonetheless the course is magnificent, it has a sensible alternation of easy and difficult holes that forces players to use every club in the bag. A lot of precision is required in order to avoid the native plants and bushes, but players are then rewarded with wide greens with fabulous backgrounds, such as the one on the 17th.

It begins with an easy par 4 of 332 yards (304 m), where attention must be paid to the water that flanks the fairway on both sides. The 5th is the hardest hole: a par 4 of 425 yards (389 m), it requires a straight drive in order to avoid all the water hazards and a good long iron to land on the well-protected green. The next hole provides a bit of a breather, but immediately after is the hardest par 3 of the course. There are water obstacles in front of and behind the hole, along with two bunkers, which make life hard even for highly skilled players, especially when playing against the wind.

The Legend

152 top With its long windows, the reception lets in the bright sunlight to make the ambience more relaxing and fresh while waiting for an aperitif or having a chat with some friends about the sports activities of the day.

152 bottom There are seven bars that act as meeting points for the guests of the Belle Mare Plage. The one in the main building has a wooden ceiling, faces the beach and the pool, has a sushi area and a cigar area. Every night guests can dance to an orchestra.

In this case a good long iron is necessary in order to reach the green. There are many memorable holes on the second nine as well. The par 4 12th is a very beautiful one, where it is advisable not to use the driver. Considering the abundance of water, it is best to be precise and then try for a par with a medium or short iron on the second shot in order to reach the long narrow green. As already mentioned the 17th hole is the most spectacular par 3 of the course, with a view of the mountains and the sea. The green is an island in the shape of a curl, but players should not be intimidated by the water. A well-placed medium iron is enough to land on the green. The hard part is trying not to do three putts. And after the great finale of the 18th (a magnificent par 5 with a slight dogleg to the right that follows a wide water hazard), you might want to relax on the sugar-white beach or in the enormous tropical garden of the Belle Mare Plage – with scenery like this, even the worst score is soon forgotten.

152-153 The atmosphere is magical by day and by night, with the large pools that lend a sense of peace and tranquility. There are seven restaurants: four between the beach and the pool two near the golf club, and one in the main building.

153 bottom Belle Mare is also a paradise for kids who, from ages 4 to 12, are entertained at the Kakoo Club. For the smaller ones there is a non-stop baby-sitting service. Naturally, one of the four swimming pools is designed for them.

153

154 The 17th hole, which stretches out onto the lagoon, is the most photographed. The Legend is open only to the guests of the Belle Mare Plage and the Prince Maurice, who can play for free.

155 top The fairways are impeccable and penetrate into the forest. The refurbished greens use Tif Dwarf grass, which easily withstands this type of climate.

155 bottom The course has the right alternation of easy and difficult holes, but always be careful to keep to the fairway, or you will need to get the ball back by venturing into the jungle or in the water. Golf carts are obligatory on both courses.

The Legend

The Legend

156-157, 156 bottom and 157 bottom It was the inauguration of the Legend, in 1994, that launched the island of Mauritius into the exclusive circle world golf destinations. Every hole of the course is unique, with different characteristics that make it memorable, requiring every club in the bag. The most important thing on Hugh Baiocchi's layout is to stay in the fairway, otherwise players will have to retrieve the ball out of the jungle or from the water. The Links was created by Rodney Wright and Peter Allis and opened in November 2002.

ASIA

Besides claiming the invention of gun powder, the compass, and paper, the Chinese now claim the invention of golf. According to the research of Professor Ling Hongling from the University of Lanzhou, a similar game has been practiced in China since the days of the Southern Tang dynasty (also known as the Nantang), which reigned from 937 to 975. The game was supposedly known as *chuiwan* and ten wooden clubs were used. These were often embellished with gold and jade insets, something that would naturally make it a rich person's pastime. According to Ling, *chuiwan* was then exported to Europe and Scotland by Mongol travelers in late Medieval times. This hypothesis may have its roots in the hazy fog of the distant past, but the more recent history of golf and how it was brought from Europe to Asia is much clearer. It was introduced into Asia more or less around 1820 by the British in India. They were far from their homeland and missed their bags, clubs, and holes. The Royal Calcutta Golf Club, founded in 1829, is the oldest one in Asia and was also the first to be established outside Britain. Twelve years later it was followed by the Royal Bombay, and so began the spread of golf throughout the orient. India became keener on cricket though, which today s considered its national sport along with field hockey.

For the next phase in the growth and then explosion of golf in Asia we have to travel eastwards to Japan. Today the Land of the Rising Sun has more than 17 million golfers second on-

ly to the United States, though it surpasses that country with its inhabitant-to-player ratio (about one to nine). The Japanese passion for golf has resulted in the construction of numerous practice courses, with multi-level facilities, as there are just not enough courses, though the numbers are growing, to allow everyone to play regularly 18 holes. Hence the extremely expensive green fees and annual membership fees that can cost tens of thousands of dollars for the most exclusive clubs outside the big cities. The golf craze also spread to South Korea (four million golfers) and Taiwan (one million), with Japanese companies building golf courses all over the region, from Indonesia to the Philippines, from Thailand to Malaysia, and all the way to Hawaii, while tour operators make millions organizing golf vacations.

China has only recently rediscovered golf, which was banished from the republic for political reasons during the days of Mao and orthodox communism. The first course was built near Beijing in the early 1980s and each year tens of new golf courses are built, and there are countless projects in the works. Given the scale of the country it is not surprising that golf is being embraced in an equally massive way. For example, Mission Hills (12 courses for a total of 216 holes) has made it into the *Guinness Book of Records* as the world's largest golf resort, surpassing America's mighty Pinehurst (eight championship courses). Meanwhile on the opposite side of Asia, the small emirate of Dubai has rapidly become an international golf center with its incredible desert courses and future plans for even more fantastic courses and golf resorts.

158 left Mission Hills has a world-record 12 courses.

158 center Another Chinese jewel: Spring City a Kunming.

158 right The Canyon Course, the best course in Thailand.

159 Graeme McDowell on the course of the Delhi Golf Club.

160-161 The aerial view shows
the difficulty of creating a course
such as the Majlis, which is
located inside the Emirates Golf
Club and is accompanied by the
interesting Wadi course. Fairways
and greens miraculously appear
out of the desert sand.

160 bottom Tiger Woods was
often a competitor in the
prestigious "Desert Classic," a
tournament of the European Tour,
which began in 1989. Other
winners, in addition to the
American champ, included
Ballesteros, Els, Couples,
Olazábal, and Montgomerie.

161 The sumptuous clubhouse
of the Emirates is the symbol of
the club: an encampment of
seven Bedouin tents formed by
crystal structures and a series of
arches. Inside there are two
restaurants, two bars, and five-
star hospitality.

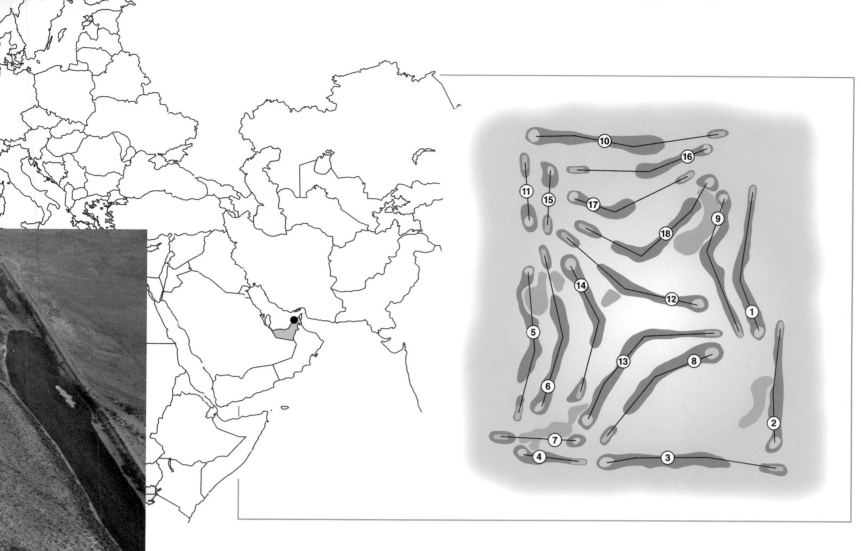

Emirates

DUBAI
(UNITED ARAB EMIRATES)

HOLE	1	2	3	4	5	6	7	8	9
YARDS	458	351	568	188	436	485	186	459	463
PAR	4	4	5	3	4	4	3	4	4

HOLE	10	11	12	13	14	15	16	17	18	TOT
YARDS	549	169	467	550	434	190	425	359	564	7301
PAR	5	3	4	5	4	3	4	4	5	72

When it was opened in 1988 the Emirates Golf Club was considered a miracle. The first grass golf course to be situated in the desert, where rain is an extremely rare event. In the Middle East golf used to be played on packed earth and sand courses. The Emirates Golf Club in contrast was a big emerald green rectangle surrounded entirely by sand and far away from any type other development or buildings. An 18-hole oasis to welcome players from northern countries who during their winters would otherwise have to stow away their bags and clubs. Just a few years on from that remarkable event, the Emirates has come to set new standards in golf. In Dubai, one of the seven states that comprise the United Arab Emirates, there are now many golf courses and many more are in the planning stages.

For several years now the extremely beautiful Majlis course (*majlis* means "meeting place") at the Emirates Golf Club has had a worthy companion, the Wadi course, which was inaugurated in 1996 and designed by Nick Faldo. All around the club there are now towering skyscrapers where once sand dunes stretched to the horizon. The person who inspired the "the miracle in the desert" was Sheikh Mohammed bin Rashid al Maktoum, who wanted a world-class course to be part of the the huge development of Dubai as an international financial center and a tourist destination. The American architect Karl Litten was hired to design it and he faced an unprecedented task. The land for the course was donated by the sheikh, who gave Litten a huge amount of money as well as precise instructions, such as the use of certain desert plants to embellish the holes.

In 1989, in order to promote this jewel on the coast of the Persian Gulf, a tournament was created that today is one of the most famous of the European professional tour, the Dubai Desert Classic. Apart from a couple of years when the tournament was held at Dubai's other equally splendid course, the Creek, the Desert Classic has always taken place on the Majlis. Many of the greatest names in the world of golf have competed, including Ballesteros, Montgomerie, Olazábal, Couples, Els, and Woods.

The white clubhouse dominating the club consists of crystal structures and a series of arches, giving it the appearance of an encampment of seven Bedouin tents. Inside the bright structures, guests will find high-class services, with two restaurants (the Classique and the Conservatory), along with the Sports Bar (which has seven screens with about 20 international sports channels) and the Spike Bar.

The dressing rooms are truly memorable, with every possible comfort. The result is five-star luxury hospitality, which starts the moment you leave your bags with the stewards at the entrance and never stops until the moment you climb back into your car to return to your hotel.

The Majlis course is a superb par 72 over 7300 yards (6600 m) and boasts many interesting holes. Two of the most challenging are the 8th and the 9th, which is a very difficult par 4 with a meandering design, bordered by sand and water that demands a delicate choice of clubs. The most beautiful par 3 is probably the 7th, which forces golfers to clear a large water hazard. This is similar to what happens on the magical 18th, a very wide par 5 protected by a lake that sprawls out in front of the green. The best players will be able to try a birdie, which is not impossible but that could turn into a disastrous score if the initial shot from the flag is not precise enough.

Framed by magnificent palms and a variety of different trees that can cope with this difficult habitat, the Majlis offers an unforgettable golfing experience, with its splendid fairways and speedy, undulating greens, interspersed among seven fresh- and salt-water lakes. As you would expect, sand is a feature on the course and there are many large bunkers, which, along with the sandy "waste areas" on the sides, remind us that the desert is never more than a par 5 away.

162-163 The Emirates Golf Club was originally isolated in the middle of the desert. The fast development of Dubai, however, has radically changed the landscape around the club in just a few years, making it reminiscent of Manhattan.

163 Tiger Woods on the 8th hole of the Majlis while competing in a Desert Classic. Bottom: the 7th and the 5th holes. The first grass golf course in the Emirates was opened in Dubai in 1988. Back then it was spoken of as a

miracle, considering how rain in the Arab Emirates is an extremely rare commodity. Today, Dubai has become a popular golf destination and new courses are constantly being planned and built.

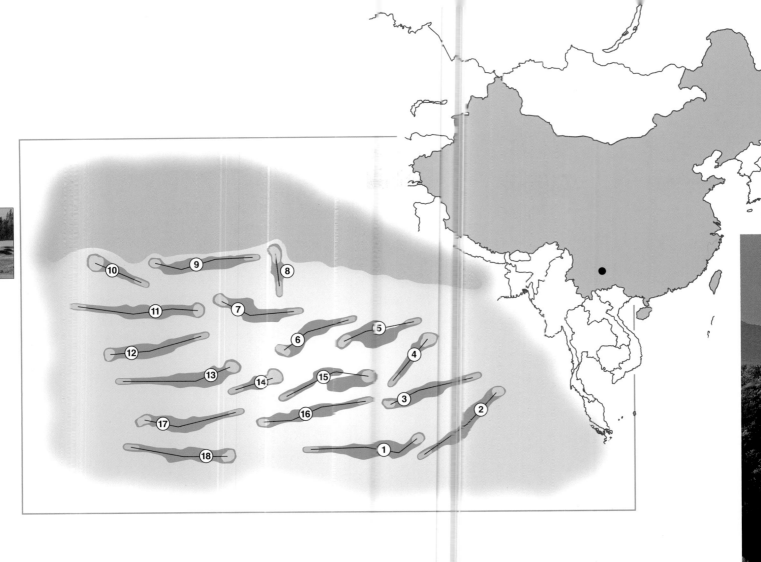

HOLE	1	2	3	4	5	6	7	8	9
YARDS	557	448	434	229	379	441	388	172	486
PAR	5	4	4	4	4	4	4	3	5

HOLE	10	11	12	13	14	15	16	17	18		TOT
YARDS	190	614	404	428	219	386	554	425	449		7203
PAR	3	5	4	4	3	4	5	4	4		73

Spring City

THE PEOPLE'S REPUBLIC OF CHINA

Kunming is China's gateway to Southeast Asia. The capital of the province of Yunnan, it is located in the southwestern region of the country and is the point of convergence for roads and railroads that from here branch out towards Myanmar (Burma), Laos, Thailand, and Vietnam. This strategic position was also very important during the Second World War and it became the transport terminus of the infamous Burma Road. Recently the decision was made to construct a highway that would connect Kunming to Chittagong (Bangladesh), passing through Myanmar.

Located at an altitude of approximately 6200 ft (1900 m) on the Yungui Plateau, at a latitude just over the Tropic of Cancer, Kunming has one of the most pleasant and temperate climates in all of China. The average temperature ranges from 50 to 68 °F (10 to 20 °C) and the thermometer never goes below 32 °F (0 °C) or rises above 77 °F (25 °C). A mild climate that makes it one of the most important international centers of commercial flower cultivation, particularly of camellias, azaleas, magnolias, primroses, lilies, and orchids, which are considered to be the six most precious jewels of the city. This is also why Kunming's nickname is "Spring City", which was chosen as the name of its famous golf club. However, the capital's greatest source of wealth is copper mining and recently the construction of a railroad link with Hanoi has expanded the area's economy. The region has also become one of the most modernized in China and in particular there has been large-scale construction of modern buildings and luxury hotels in order to develop the tourism industry.

One of Kunming's attractions is the great Lake Dian, which has a surface area of almost 115 sq miles (300 sq km). It is famous throughout China and inspired Emperor Qianlong, who lived during the 18th century, to commission what today is known as Kunming Hù, the artificial lake of the Summer Palace in Beijing.

164 Spring City is the name the Chinese gave to Kunming, the capital of Yunnan province, because of its pleasant weather conditions.

164-165 One of the most beautiful holes of the Lake Course at Kunming, designed by Robert Trent Jones Jr., is the 2nd, a par 4 of 448 yards (410 m).

165 bottom The large water hazard is the main adversary on the 13th hole of the Mountain Course, an intriguing par 3 of 180 yards (165 m).

166 top and bottom There are
two 18-hole courses at Spring
City, designed by two famous
American architects, Jack
Nicklaus (with 18 Major wins in
his career) and Robert Trent
Jones Jr.

166-167 and 167 Robert Trent
Jones Jr. chose the area near
Lake Yang Zong Hai for his Lake
Course. There is a marked
difference in the levels between
the holes around the clubhouse
and the ones near the lake,
which from the 8th to the 11th
offer a magnificent panorama of
the lake.

Spring City

names in golf design. The first course, the Mountain Course, was assigned to Jack Nicklaus who, after having set the record of 18 major championships in his career, started designing courses at the highest level. In Kunming, the legendary golfer relied on the rolling terrain to design a course with many raised tees and greens within a landscape dominated by the lake and large pines. Wide fairways allow the use of a driver without too many worries. Thanks to its altitude of 6890 ft (2100 m) the ball flies farther than usual. To counter this, the bunkers and the grassy hollows can be troublesome if you are less than precise when approaching the

This artificial lake took approximately 10,000 laborers four years to construct. The characteristics of Kunming make it easy to understand why the Keppel Group (one of Singapore's biggest international corporations) chose it for one of its first resort developments in China. In fact Spring City Golf and Lake Resort has already celebrated its first ten years – it was built in 1998. The resort on the shores of Lake Yang Zong Hai (smaller and more intimate than Lake Dian) proudly boasted the first course that introduced golf to China after decades of obstruction by the communist regime.

This gorgeous project, which combines luxury villas with two 18-hole courses, was the creation of two prestigious

green. Mention must be made of the 8th and 13th holes, which are rather short, delicate par 3s, except for the presence of water hazards, and the amazing 18th. As a "signature hole," Nicklaus chose the hardest and longest par 4 as the sweeping finale for this delightful course. Then we have the Lake Course designed by Robert Trent Jones Jr. The two main characteristics of this course are the remarkable height difference of nearly 460 ft (140 m) between the holes around the clubhouse and those beside the lake, and its impressive length of 7203 yards (6586 m). The view of Lake Yang Zong Hai is particularly spectacular from the difficult 8th to the 11th holes.

168-169 On the course designed by Nicklaus in Spring City, the Mountain Course has ample fairways that allow for a easy drive, such as the 11th hole, a nice par 4 of 387 yards (354 m).

Spring City

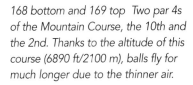

168 bottom and 169 top Two par 4s
of the Mountain Course, the 10th and
the 2nd. Thanks to the altitude of this
course (6890 ft/2100 m), balls fly for
much longer due to the thinner air.

169 bottom As a signature hole,
Nicklaus chose the 18th hole, a
long and challenging par 4,
which makes a stunning finish
for this delightful course.

170-171 The 15th hole is the most significant of the Olazábal Course, a sharp left dogleg with a large lake and an impressive series of bunkers near the landing area.

170 bottom It is probably the most challenging final hole of all the Mission Hills courses, a long par 4 of 460 yards (421 m). The water follows the 18th hole from the starting tee to the green.

171 top Water is used for various purposes: an obstacle to challenge players or a waterfall to please the eyes of those who wander near the clubhouse, which stands as a background for the 18th.

171 bottom With its 7355 yards (6725 m), the Olazábal Course is the longest of the 12 courses at Mission Hills. Among its distinctive characteristics are the bunkers with different contorted "fingers," vertical walls, and concave floors.

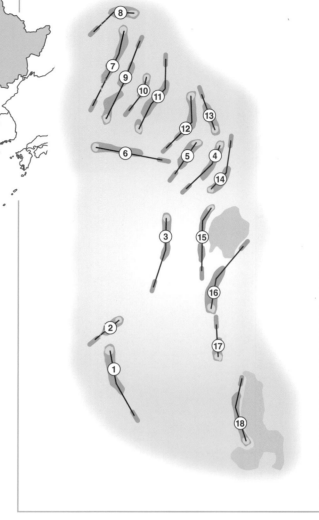

Mission Hills

THE PEOPLE'S REPUBLIC OF CHINA

The modernization of China has been spectacularly fast. No one would have ever imagined that the China of 40 years ago would change so dramatically that it would now be able to boast an entry in the *Guinness World Book of Records* for a mega-resort, consisting of 11 championship courses and an 18-hole executive course (a total of 216 holes) – as advertised by the billboards along the 31-mile (50-km) freeway from Hong Kong airport to the gates of Mission Hills.

Mission Hills is an invention of Dr. Chu, who in 1992 imagined the largest and most opulent golf resort in the world. He chose an area of 6.9 sq miles (18 sq km) between the cities of Shenzhen and Dongguan. The other marvels of this club include the world's largest pro shop, a fun park for children, Asia's largest tennis complex with 51 courts, a 315-room five-star hotel, and four spas. Not to mention that one of its clubhouses covers an area of 300,000 sq ft (28,000 sq m), the 3000 caddies (all female) in red tracksuits, and a huge fleet of golf carts. Twelve courses have been designed by the greatest course architects and the most famous international players from nine countries. Behind it all is a single Arizona company that created the master plan and played an integral role in the landscaping of each course – Schmidt-Curley Design. They literally leveled mountains in order to realize the different terrains required by the designers. The background scenery and countryside are basically the same for all the courses, that is, thick jungle and large trees. What differentiates them is the architecture of the landscape, the types of grass, the shapes of the tees, and the styles of the bunkers.

The first course, which opened in 1994, is the World Cup Course by Jack Nicklaus, and the first to be accredited by the PGA in China. It hosted the 1995 World Cup. We then have the projects by Ernie Els, Nick Faldo, Jumbo Ozaki, and Vijay Singh. From 2003 to 2004 the courses designed by David Duval, David Leadbetter, Annika Sorenstam (the only woman), Greg Norman, and José María Olazábal were inaugurated. In 2007 the last two courses were opened, which were created by Pete Dye and the first 18 par 3 holes in China designed by Zhang Lian Wei. The easiest to play are the courses by Leadbetter, Duval, and Sorenstam.

HOLE	1	2	3	4	5	6	7	8	9
YARDS	447	175	548	441	176	476	565	214	573
PAR	4	3	5	4	3	4	5	3	5

HOLE	10	11	12	13	14	15	16	17	18		TOT
YARDS	404	568	457	241	401	580	432	197	460		7355
PAR	4	5	4	3	4	5	4	3	4		72

ASIA

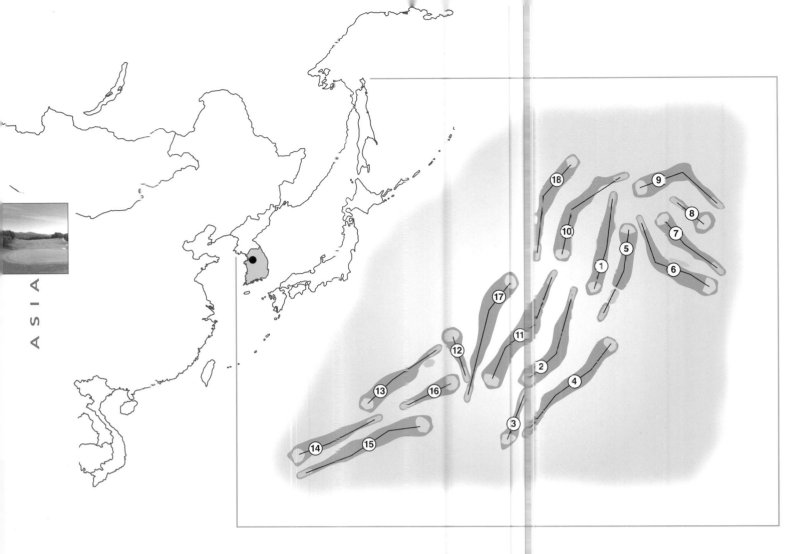

Newseoul

SOUTH KOREA

HOLE	1	2	3	4	5	6	7	8	9
YARDS	404	393	207	494	402	430	334	191	390
PAR	4	4	3	5	4	5	4	3	4

HOLE	10	11	12	13	14	15	16	17	18		TOT
YARDS	346	471	207	392	362	512	208	353	395		6495
PAR	4	5	3	4	4	5	3	4	4		72

According to the latest data from the IGF (International Golf Federation) there are four million golfers in South Korea, out of a population of about 50 million. An extremely high number of golfers compared to the country's limited number of golf courses. In the whole of South Korea there are less than 300 courses, which leads to massive overcrowding and a demand that cannot be satisfied. Korean golfers, along with the Japanese, are therefore enthusiastic golf tourists, as demonstrated by their millions of trips abroad to enjoy their favorite sport. The result is that two billion dollars are spent abroad, which has caused the government to seriously consider the possibility of quickly increasing the number of courses to reduce the vast amount of revenue lost to the country. Green fees and membership fees in Korea are some of the highest in the world, even higher than those in Japan. The ever-growing passion for golf has a series of positive implications, such as the many Korean players' associations scattered all over the world and especially the great results achieved in competitions. Of the male players Kyung-Ju Cho (aka K.J. Choi) can boast many victories on the PGA Tour, while there are almost 50 Korean female pros who are permanently involved in golf competitions (only the United States has more). Some of the most successful women are Se Ri Pak, the national number one, Gloria and Grace Park, Mi Hyun Kim, and Hee-Won Han. An impressive lineup and fearsome adversaries of champions like the Mexican Lorena Ochoa and Annika Sorenstam from Sweden.

Although in Korea at the moment there are not enough clubs to satisfy demand, there are many excellent courses, such as the 36 holes of the Newseoul Country Club, which was founded in 1987 in Kwangiu, about 18 miles (30 km) south-east of the capital, Seoul.

174 In South Korea there are less than 300 courses, very few compared to the almost four million golfers. Among the most prestigious clubs in the country is the Newseoul Country Club, Kwangiu.

174-175 The 36 holes of the Newseoul Country Club are among the most interesting in all of South Korea. The club was founded in 1987 in Kwangiu, about 18 miles (30 km) south-east of Seoul.

175 top The clubhouse of the
Newseoul Country Club serves
two 18-hole courses, the North
Course and the South Course,
which every year are visited by
160,000 players.

Newseoul

Every year, about 160,000 players visit the club, which stretches out over a gorgeous area of 630 acres (255 hectares) within a vast natural forest. There are two courses with different technical characteristics. The North Course, a par 72 of 6495 yards (5939 m), requires courage and strategy to play its wide, very curvy fairways and the great variety of different perspectives they offer a player. The course is in perfect harmony with the surrounding nature, which manages to camouflage the course's difficulty. The South Course, a par 72 of 6321 yards (5780 m), is more approachable and less lively. The greens on both courses are superb and there are about 150 well-placed bunkers, which bring players back to reality after a poor shot. Luckily the beauty of nature and the surrounding views are enough to make you forget your mistakes.

176 The North Course is the most challenging course of the Newseoul Country Club, which covers about 630 acres (255 hectares) of gently rolling countryside.

176-177 and 177 bottom The North Course is a par 72 of 6495 yards (5939 m) and is a challenging course that requires courage and strategy to play, though its toughness is well camouflaged by the scenery.

Newseoul

178 The South Course of the Newseoul Country Club is easier compared to its challenging North companion. The terrain is less irregular, but with some pleasant and diverting water hazards. The South Course measures 6321 yards (5780 m) and is an excellent course, much like the rest of the courses in Korea. In recent years great progress has been made at the competitive level, with champions such as K. J. Choi and women pros such as the excellent Se Ri Pak.

*178-179 and 179 bottom
One of the most noticeable characteristics of the Newseoul Country Club are the greens, which are magnificent. A mention must also be made of the 150 bunkers scattered throughout the North Course and the South Course, which are capable of giving ant player a hard time.*

180-181 The South African Ernie Els on the 6th hole during the third round of the 2008 Indian Masters. In February 2008 the Delhi Golf Club debuted on the European Tour, becoming a venue for this event with its 2.5 million dollar prize.

180 bottom The crowd awaits the arrival of the pros on the 18th hole. For years the course has hosted the Indian Open, a tournament of the Asian PGA Tour. The club, which opened in 1931, is the oldest of the capital. Its origin dates back to when the capital of India was moved from Calcutta to Delhi.

181 Shiv Shankar Prasad Chowrasia, the Indian player at the top of the list of the Asian Tour, on the fairway of the 18th. He won the Indian Masters in front of a home audience.

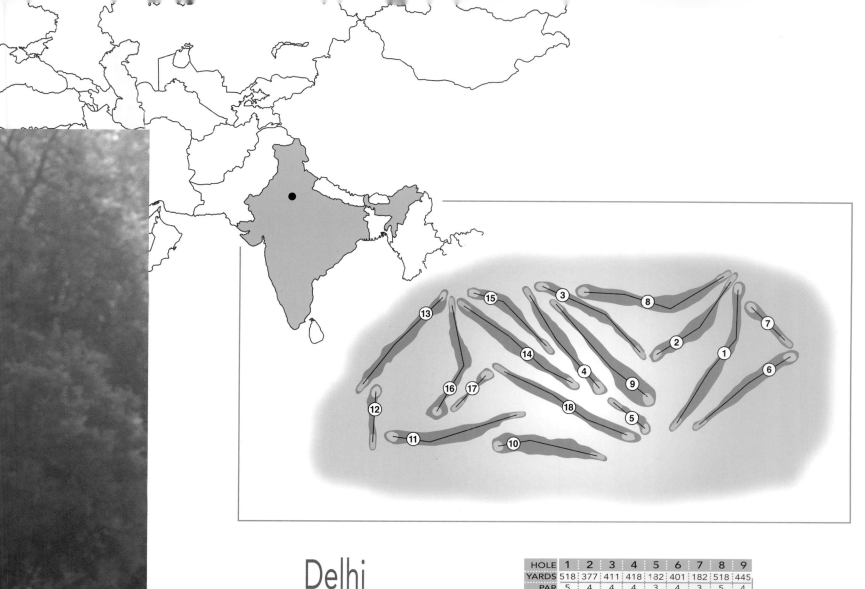

Delhi

INDIA

HOLE	1	2	3	4	5	6	7	8	9
YARDS	518	377	411	418	182	401	182	518	445
PAR	5	4	4	4	3	4	3	5	4

HOLE	10	11	12	13	14	15	16	17	18		TOT
YARDS	428	437	188	386	516	353	412	165	545		6882
PAR	4	4	3	4	5	4	4	3	5		72

Perhaps not everyone knows that India is the first country after Great Britain to have developed golf as a sport and so it has some of the oldest courses in the world outside of Europe. The Delhi Club, which dates back to 1931, is the course that for years hosted the Indian Open, which is part of the Asian PGA Tour, and then has become the venue for the Indian Masters, the only leg of the European Tour in India. The capital's oldest club represents a dive into the past with a series of holes through the tombs of an ancient dynasty, which has its origins in the beginning of the century, when the decision was made to move India's capital from Calcutta to Delhi. Two British architects, Sir Edwin Landseer Lutyens and Sir Herbert Baker were hired to create a new capital that was a worthy addition to the ancient city of Delhi, and in 1928 New Delhi officially came into being.

Sir Edwin decided that golf in New Delhi had to be played in a better area than the one where the two courses of the day were located. The search for a new location as well as its construction was entrusted to the head of the Department of Horticulture, a Scotsman with a passion for golf and archeology. With the aid of a pair of elephants, he traveled through the thick jungle until he reached the area where, in 1473, the army of King Lodhi of Delhi had attacked the forces of King Hussein of Jaunpore. The area then became a huge burial site for Moghul nobles. The Scotsman thought it was the ideal spot, mainly because it was so full of

fascinating hidden remains, which could well prove intriguing distractions if uncovered by an unfortunate player trying to "dig" his way out of a bunker. Thus began the Lochi Golf Club. However, the club struggled to survive due to the small number of members and the lack of water that made green maintenance difficult. The commencement of the Second World War brought a change for the better, because the course was suddenly teeming with military personnel.

Every effort was made to keep standards high and nine extra holes were built to accommodate the now abundant golfers. With the end of the war came the partitioning of India, which resulted in a drastic reduction in members and a subsequent lack of funds to maintain the course. Somehow the club managed to survive and in 1951 it was renamed Delhi Golf Club.

Delhi

By now it was no longer in the middle of the jungle but had been absorbed into the ever-growing urban sprawl that today is home to 15 million people. Inevitably, developers began to covet this green oasis and the prime minister had to intervene in order to guarantee a multi-year lease.

In 1977-78 the course was redesigned by Peter Thompson, who kept the thick vegetation, the curving fairways, and the original deep bunkers. There then followed a period of consolidation, and it became one of the most attractive and most visited courses in the country. The location is extraordinary, right

in the heart of a massive metropolis. In keeping with parkland style, the course lacks water hazards but is rich with trees beside the fairways and thorny bushes that make up the rough. All this requires precise shots. In fact very few players use the driver on this course, which from the starting championship tees exceeds 6800 yards (6200 m). The tee of the 4th hole is dominated by a Lodhi tomb with a cupola roof, which was restored in 1998, and there are another eight tombs scattered throughout the course, giving it a truly historical atmosphere.

182 top The Danish Thomas Björn has just taken the tee shot from the 4th hole. He must have been surprised to find a beautiful tomb that was recently restored to its former splendor.

182 bottom Birdwatchers have a lot to watch in the green area that encloses the Delhi Golf Club: in fact this reserve hosts over 300 different species of birds.

182-183 It is common to find players wearing a turban on the greens of the Delhi Golf Club. Here, golf has been played for a long time, because India's first courses were built by the British in the 19th century. It is home to some of the world's oldest courses outside Europe.

183 bottom With baskets full of sand on their head, the women in charge of the divots come to do their job when too much soil is removed. The club is no longer in the middle of the jungle as it was when it was created, now it is surrounded by a vast metropolis of 15 million people.

184-185 The 16th hole is a short par 4 with its green surrounded by round-edged bunkers. The yellow color of the grass should come as no surprise. The water crisis affecting the whole world involves golf, too.

185 top Before the course was built, the fairway of the 13th hole probably housed a railroad station.

185 bottom For years the Delhi Golf Club has hosted the Indian Open, part of the Asian Tour. It is also a venue for the Indian Masters. The original course was redesigned in 1976–77 by Peter Thompson and some holes were radically changed. A nine-hole course was also built.

Delhi

186-187 The 14th hole, with its gorgeous view, is characteriyed by a raised tee overlooking the island green.

186 bottom From the championship tees on the 18th (a par 4), players must make it over the water, but even from the forward tees it is advisable to play it safe and stay on the left.

187 The insignia of the club incorporates natural motifs, in a similar way the course harmonizes with nature too, following the philosophy of the architect Yoshikazu Kato.

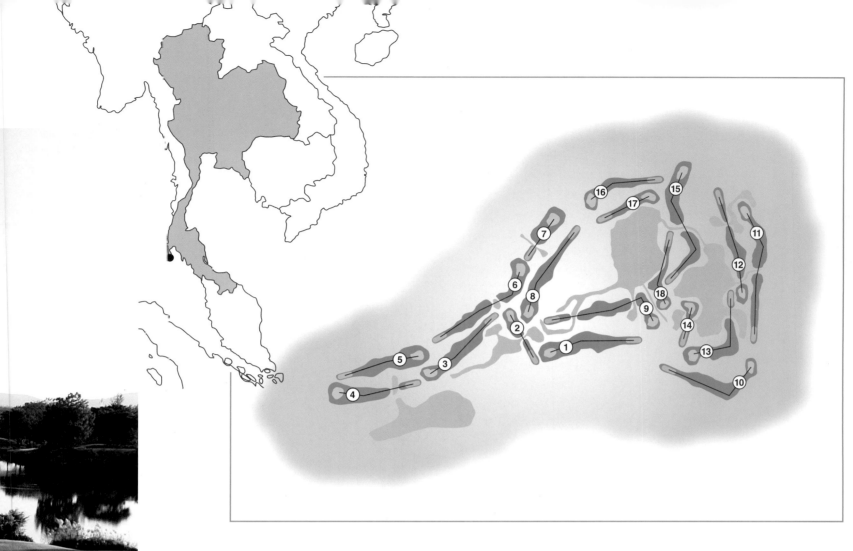

Blue Canyon

THAILAND

HOLE	1	2	3	4	5	6	7	8	9
YARDS	390	218	449	407	398	556	205	412	561
PAR	4	3	4	4	4	5	3	4	5

HOLE	10	11	12	13	14	15	16	17	18		TOT
YARDS	392	600	440	390	194	586	357	221	403		7179
PAR	4	5	4	4	3	5	4	3	4		72

Phuket, the "pearl of the South," is a gem of a Thai island, a paradise with lush vegetation and abundant natural resources. It is a hugely popular tourist destination and has lately become a golf center too. The most renowned club on the is and is the Blue Canyon, which covers 716 acres (290 hectares) of a very green valley bordered by the Phang Nga mountains and the Andaman Sea. It has two championship courses, the Canyon and the Lakes Course.

As soon as it was opened in 1991, the first course became a legend and established itself as one of the best courses in the region. The designer was Yoshikazu Kato, who became famous for his architectonic philosophy. In fact Kato refused to settle for an artificial design and patiently carved out a course from what the land still had to offer after its despoliation by a rubber plantation and tin mines. The course is uniquely integrated into and characterized by the environment and has natural hazards, such as huge tropical vegetation, canyons, and bodies of water on ten of its holes that manage to intimidate players of all levels. It is a masterpiece that has been described as the best golf retreat designed by nature and the most difficult golf in Asia.

The outward holes penetrate into what was the rubber plantation, while the much more open return holes follow the water, which even fills the ancient quarries. There are many exceptional holes, which you will never forget even if you play the course only once. For example, the 3rd is the longest par 4 of 448 yards (410 m) from the championship tee, with a narrow uphill fairway lined by trees. Influencing the game are, on the second shot, the gigantic Calabash tree in the middle of the fairway and, on the last shot, the position of the flag on the long green. The raised tees at the 10th hole provide an excellent view not only of the hole, with its abrupt left dogleg, but also of the bay of Phang Nga. Rubber trees line the fairway and there is a succession of six bunkers from the elbow to the green, which is protected on the right and on the back.

The hardest hole is the 11th, a par 5 of 600 yards (549 m), where the tee shot should reach close to the water that crosses the fairway, possibly on the right. From this position players are guaranteed a better landing area for their next shot. The right club selection and the precision of the shot are essential for the approach to the long green, which has bunkers and water on both sides. The most spectacular holes are the 13th, a par 4 of 390 yards (357 m)

Blue Canyon

188 top *The second nine are much wider but feature various lakes (mine shafts filled with water)*

188 bottom *The Canyon Course is considered one of the most difficult of Asian courses. It is impossible to obtain a decent score if you do not play well*

whose tee shot must fly over a canyon (more impressive than tricky), and the 14th, which has a beautiful view from the raised tee that overlooks the island green. This green can be fatal if players misjudge the distance or choose the wrong club.

Yoshikazu Kato has made Blue Canyon his home residence and calls the two courses "my two sons," while members refer to the Canyon Course as the "Blue Nasty." Rather than nasty it is extremely challenging and is the first course to host the Johnnie Walker Classic twice, making it a legend. For the first time, in 1994, Tiger Woods played as an amateur and finished 34th despite his 71, which is still the beginner's record for the course, one shot under the course's par. The second time Woods played, in 1998, he returned as a professional and won an exciting matchplay with Ernie Els. Any amateur who can do better than Woods on this course should probably start playing professionally and will probably become the next world number one.

188-189 In addition to a precise drive, the course demands excellent putts, because the greens are extremely fast and rolling.

189 bottom The first nine holes are bordered by the former rubber plantation, so they are narrow and surrounded by trees.

190-191 On the 4th, a par 4 of
407 yards (363 m), the drive must
clear the small hills 200 ft (80 m)
from the championship tees to
avoid a blind shot to the green,
which is protected by bunkers.

191 top The name of the course
comes from the course's many
canyons. Members call it the
"Blue Nasty" for the effort it
requires.

191 bottom Tiger Woods when
he played as an amateur here in
the 1994 Johnnie Walker Classic
and still holds the amateur record
of 71.

Blue Canyon

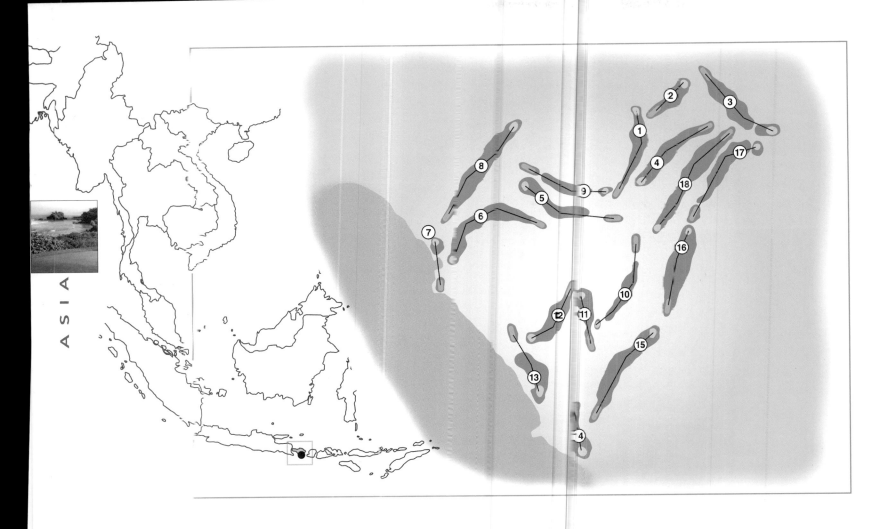

HOLE	1	2	3	4	5	6	7	8	9
YARDS	383	188	400	439	441	501	214	544	388
PAR	4	3	4	4	4	5	3	5	4

HOLE	10	11	12	13	14	15	16	17	18	TOT
YARDS	445	211	381	337	186	447	431	349	520	6805
PAR	5	3	4	4	3	4	4	4	5	72

Nirwana Bali

INDONESIA

198 The 18 holes of the Nirwana are situated in an award-winning resort, managed by the Le Méridien hotel chain, sprawling over 247 acres (100 hectares) of land and framed by volcano peaks and the sea.

199 The gorgeous lush vegetation is the greatest feature of the Nirwana Golf Club, an incredibly fascinating course designed by the legendary Australian player Greg Norman on the southern coast of the island of Bali.

Gorgeous caddies, a picturesque sea, rice paddies, lush green hills, and in the background the temple of Tanah Lot, appearing to be suspended above the waves. A paradise of a setting located on the southern coast of Bali, offers golfers hours of spectacular play that can be equalled by few other courses in the world. Naturally, this is the Nirwana Golf Club, the name of which is almost identical to the word nirvana which was used by the Buddha to describe the perfect peace of mind, free from passion, disturbance, bonds, and any type of affliction. Definitely not a casual choice as this piece of heaven seems to have been carved out of the island to make people forget all their worldly concerns.

Considered by many critics to be the most beautiful course in Asia, it was designed by the great Greg Norman, who never concealed his pride in being the author of such a masterpiece. "I must be honest, every golf architect would love to have the perfect landscape at his disposal to translate into a wonderful course. In Bali, I was just that lucky." Norman's jewel is set in an award-winning resort, managed by the Le Méridien chain, which sprawls out over 247 acres (100 hectares) and is framed by volcanic peaks (the highest of which is the still active Agung at 10,308 ft/3142 m). The vegetation, which includes palms, plantations, and green terraces for the cultivation of rice, is lush to say the least. Fairly close are the tourist cities of Kuta and Kegian, while Denpasar is 15 miles (25 km) away.

... the Johnnie Walker Classic in 1994 and in 1998. Paul Casey (born in England but living in Arizona) is not the only player to have to deal with the bunker on the 18th.

very demanding par 3 with a water obstacle on the left and large bunkers guarding the fast green. It is advisable to observe the trees to judge the force and direction of the wind.

This city is the capital of the island of Bali, which is one of the over 17,500 islands that make up the world's largest archipelago that is the nation of Indonesia. A few degrees south of the equator, Bali is a tiny Hindu enclave of about three million people, who follow the rituals of the oldest of the great religions in their characteristic, colored temples.

The Nirwana Golf Club is situated in one of the island's most beautiful areas and is managed and kept in perfect shape by the experienced International Management Group,

the largest international sports marketing company. To play the 18 holes designed by the "Great White Shark" you need to use a car while almost obligatory, though pleasant, is the presence of the Balinese caddies, who give an extra touch of class and uniqueness to the whole setting. The course begins by unfolding out among rice paddies, palms, and the thick tropical forest that surrounds the hotel. Only from the 6th hole, a nice par 5 with a marked left dogleg, do you start breathing ocean air, which literally explodes onto the following hole. The marvelous 7th, the signature hole of the Nirwana Golf Club, is an unforgettable par 3 played from one cliff to the other, shooting over the Indian Ocean and hoping the wind won't slow or alter the trajectory. In fact, the ball must fly far because the hole is almost 220 yards (200 m). On

the horizon, is the incredible silhouette of the temple of Tanah Lot. Also amazing are the 13th hole, a par 4 played along the water, and the 14th, where the ocean is once again a major feature and even laps the starting tee. One single, well-adjusted shot brings us from the beach to the raised green on the cliffs. Only 186 yards (170 m) long, yet the magic of the scenery seems to make it even longer and quite unforgettable.

Nirwana Bali

200 and 200-201 The temple of Tanah Lot, in the middle of the sea, is the background for the signature hole of the Nirwana, the 7th, a par 3 of 214 yards (196 m), where the ball must fly

over the Indian Ocean. The course unfolds among rice paddies, palms, and thick tropical brush, and three of its holes are played only a few steps from the sea.

201 The course designed by Greg Norman starts inland, among the rice paddies, palms, and thick tropical vegetation. From the 6th hole, a nice par 5

with a marked left dogleg, players start breathing the ocean air. The course requires the use of the cart and a Balinese caddy.

OCEANIA

Golf in Oceania is limited almost exclusively to Australia and New Zealand. This is largely because of the amount of land available to build courses (most of Oceania is made up of islands) and the great historical influence that Britain had on the emerging nations of Australia and New Zealand, which inevitably involved sporting traditions. Today, there are 1.1 million members of Golf Australia and 1600 courses in this island-continent, which makes it the world's fifth golfing nation. The excellence of Australian golf is clearly demonstrated by Peter Thomson's five victories at the British Open Championship between 1954 and 1965, by the legendary Greg Norman's two victories in the same competition, and David Graham's double victory in the U.S. Open and the PGA Championship. There have been four other Aussie victories in the Grand Slams, the last one belonging to Geoff Ogilvy, who won the 2006 U.S. Open and is one of the stars of the new wave of Australian pros, along with Robert Allenby, Stuart Appleby, and Adam Scott (the author of this book's preface).

Australia's golf history actually begins in Tasmania, the large island-state 150 miles (240 km) south of Melbourne. The Bothwell Golf Club was founded in 1839 and the first course to be constructed in this region of the world was designed by a Scotsman, Alexander Reid. After a two-year trip back to Scotland, Reid returned to Australia fully equipped with precious down-stuffed cowhide balls, ready to spread the gospel of golf. Eight years after the first chunks of grass were "chopped up" in Tasmania, golf was being played even in the heart of Melbourne, at Flagstaff Gardens. Soon after, attempts at golf were made in Sydney and Adelaide, even though the construction of more or less official courses never proved that successful and usually the courses only lasted a few seasons. And so began the hundred-year-old dispute between the two most prestigious Australian clubs to determine which deserves the title of the oldest club in the country. The contenders are the Australian in Sydney and the Royal Melbourne. The former was established in 1882 and six years later it lost the course until 1895, while the latter was founded in 1891 but its club and course remained in continual use.

In New Zealand there are almost 500,000 players, 125,000 of which hold an official N.Z. Golf Handicap. There are about 420 courses, with green fees ranging from 10 NZ dollars for simple public courses to just under 100 NZ dollars for the more classy, exclusive ones. The country's golf "hero" is Michael Campbell, the winner of the 2005 U.S. Open and the first New Zealander to win a Major. He is of Maori origin and was also elected sportsman of the year, becoming as famous as the All Blacks rugby team and the yachtsmen who won the America's Cup. As far as the rest of this ocean-scattered continent is concerned, there are another two nations that are members of the International Golf Federation: Papua New Guinea (15 courses and 3000 golfers) and the Cook Islands. However, a few beautiful courses can be found in Polynesia and Micronesia as well.

202 left The spectacle of Cape Kidnappers, New Zealand.

202 right The fascinating clubhouse at Royal Melbourne.

203 One of the symbols of golf in Australia, the New South Wales.

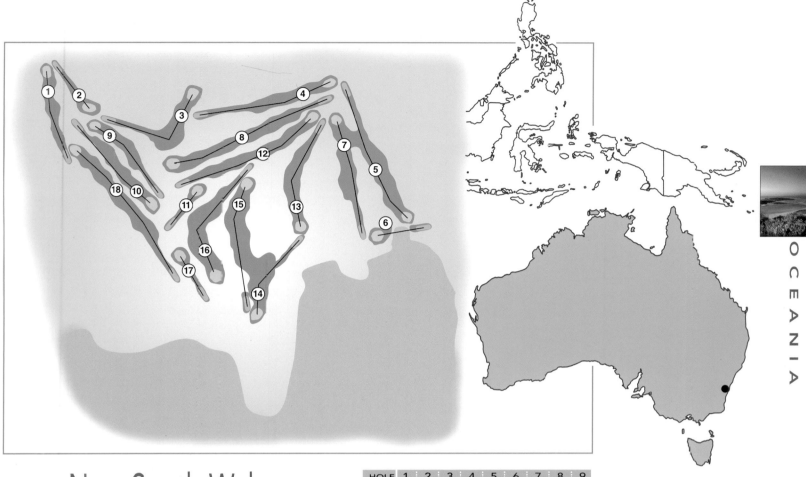

New South Wales

AUSTRALIA

HOLE	1	2	3	4	5	6	7	8	9
YARDS	320	201	416	428	514	194	411	552	372
PAR	4	3	4	4	5	3	4	5	4

HOLE	10	11	12	13	14	15	16	17	18		TOT
YARDS	394	163	527	410	353	407	441	167	548		6818
PAR	4	3	5	4	4	4	4	3	5		72

As a medical doctor, Dr. Alister MacKenzie thought that for many of his patients the best medicine was golf. He then decided that it was also good for himself, so he left his profession and, although he never became a really good player, became one of the best golf architects ever (even though, as often happens, his work was only appreciated after his death). Born in England in 1870, he died in 1934 in California. During his life he designed more than 400 courses, of which the most spectacular is in New South Wales on the northern cape of Botany Bay, about 20 minutes from downtown Sydney. It rivals his other masterpiece, Cypress Point. Even though Australian fairways are less smooth, the view of the ocean is better than the ones at Cypress Point and Pebble Beach, the two California giants – and you can also watch whales.

MacKenzie was hired along with Alex Russell to take care of the new layout of the Royal Melbourne, but stayed only three months (from October to December 1926). However, he was so enthralled by the vast landscapes that he managed to obtain other assignments in Australia and when he finally left he had created some of the country's finest courses. The most characteristic is this 1928 course, the New South Wales, which stretches out dramatically among capes and valleys on the edge of the jaggy Pacific coast. It is has a notable connection with the past, because the site of the 18th tee is where Captain Cook found the first drinkable water source. It also immerses a player in nature. Playing here means playing golf as it was originally conceived, using your skill against the hazards created by nature. The course is bordered on three sides by water and has many characteristics of a links and certainly the wind is always a dominant factor. With a light breeze it appears as calm as a sleeping volcano (even though the narrow, curving fairways and the small greens can already

204 The clubhouse, recently renovated, is a beautiful fusion of traditional architecture and luxurious features. It offers splendid glimpses of the course and the ocean, which is the backdrop for the 17th and 18th holes.

205 The coat of arms of the New South Wales Golf Club is the same as the state of New South Wales: a rising sun over a golden lion and kangaroo, with a shield and the motto Orta recens quam pura nites.

206-207 The 13th, a par 4 with a left dogleg that features a treeless bend, allows a player to choose one of two game options: an aggressive or a more conservative style.

207 top The large bunkers do not diminish the charm of the 6th hole, the most photographed par 3 in Australia. Starting from the blue tees perched on the reef is a truly electrifying experience.

207 bottom Another breathtaking hole with a view of the ocean, where a player must take into consideration the height difference left of the green as well as the bunkers on both sides.

test medium-level players), but when the wind breaks loose it is like an eruption and really tests players' powers and ability. The little time he spent in Australia did not allow MacKenzie to finalize all the details of the course, and in 1932 Eric Appleby became involved in order to complete the design of the bunkers and to make a few necessary modifications to the holes. The highly praised 6th hole was added by him, but in compliance with MacKenzie's principles and perfectly in keeping with the original concept. It is the landscape that shapes the holes and not the other way around. It is more exciting to play on crests and overhanging rocks than on valleys. Therefore, the player must face hills and crests from every possible angle. Every hole is unique and worthy of mention, but certain ones in particular have made New South Wales a temple of golf. We can only mention two here for reasons of space. The first

is the 5th, a par 5 of 514 yards (470 m). From the tee all you can see is a crest in the fairway, which prevents you from seeing the landing zone, instead you have a view of the ocean and the horizon. This makes for an aesthetically breathtaking hole but a technically difficult one, considering that, in addition to the blind shot, there is still a 165 ft (50 m) second shot. The second hole to mention is the 6th, a par 3 of 194 yards (177 m). This is Australia's most photographed hole and goes in the opposite direction of the previous hole. Starting from the white tee or the blue tee makes a difference. If you choose the blue, perched atop the reef and accessible via a small bridge, it is one of the most exciting shots ever. From the white tee on the mainland, the hole is simpler, even though the small green is defended by a slope on the left and by a series of bunkers.

HOLE	1	2	3	4	5	6	7	8	9		TOT
YARDS	429	480	354	470	176	428	148	379	416		
PAR	4	5	4	5	3	4	3	4	4		
HOLE	10	11	12	13	14	15	16	17	18		
YARDS	305	455	476	147	366	167	221	439	433		6589
PAR	4	4	5	3	4	5	3	4	4		72

Royal Melbourne

AUSTRALIA

The Royal title was given to the club by Queen Victoria in 1895 and Australia's most prestigious course still bears it with pride and deservedly so, thanks to two extraordinarily beautiful courses, the East and West. The Royal Melbourne Golf Club touches Port Phillip Bay, a huge circular bay that protects the city of Melbourne from the big seas of the Bass Strait, which stretches for 150 miles (240 km) between Tasmania and Australia. Since the first half of the 19th century, courses were built in the main urban centers of the country and golf arrived in Melbourne in 1847. The first, very natural courses were built quickly, but just as quickly they were replaced with farmland, cattle stations, or industry. The first choice for the Royal Melbourne was an area near Caulfield Railway Station. It was 1891 and the club was incorporated on 22 May at the Scott's Hotel in Melbourne, with an assembly that elected Sir James McBain as president. The club had 73 members. After only six weeks the course was inaugurated and it measured 4750 yards (4343 m). The following year women were allowed to become members of the club, which was well ahead of its time as far as equal rights are concerned.

Due to problems encountered with the construction of new residential neighborhoods, the club was forced to move to a new location only a few years later. The new location was chosen during a picnic and was about 7 miles (12 km) from Caulfield at a place called Black Rock, which today is part of a suburb south of Melbourne. The location was destined to become the temple of golf in the sixth-largest nation of the world, though the least densely populated with only two people per square kilometer.

210 Considered the first golf club in Australia, the Royal Melbourne has hosted a long series of important tournaments on the "Composite Course," which merges 12 holes of the West with six of the East.

210-211 and 211 bottom The Royal Melbourne Golf Club, with its historic 36 holes, touches the shores of the enormous Port Phillip Bay. The founding of the club dates back to 22nd May 1891.

NORTH AMERICA

The golf statistics for the U.S. are astonishing: there are between 26 and 27 million golfers, more or less half of all the golfers in the world, with about 16,000 courses at their disposal, an impressive number that greatly increased during the 1990s when some 500 new courses were built each season. The tragedy of 11th September 2001 halted the expansion of golf in the States, which still remains the fourth most popular sport in the country after football, baseball, and basketball, though it is perhaps less rigorously played than in Europe. In fact, only a small percentage of American golfers have a clean handicap. Most players do not take part in matches but prefer playing a nice game with friends.

The history of golf in North America begins in the late 19th century in Hastings-on-Hudson, slightly north of New York. The St. Andrew's Golf Club claims to be the first club on American soil and also claims that in 1888 a Scottish sportsman, John Reid, started hitting a few balls with a group of friends in front of some unruffled cows. The first course had only three holes and the "clubhouse" was an old apple tree where gentlemen in jacket, cap, and knickerbockers would hang their clothes and their flasks of fine scotch whisky. The club has stayed active since those days, earning the title of the oldest club in the United States. In 1894 the USGA (United States Golf Association) was founded, and the following year the first U.S. Open took place at the Newport Country Club, Rhode Island. Victory went to an Englishman, Horace Rawlins, who defeated a field of over ten opponents. From then on golf took huge strides, making

the U.S. one of the leading nations in golf. In every one of the 50 States there are mind-blowing courses, and, in some states more than others, golf has become a true industry. For example, Florida (the only state with more than 1000 courses), Arizona, California, the two Carolinas, and Hawaii, where golf usually accompanies amusement parks and beach resorts.

In the United States golf is also a great tradition, which often means ultra-private, unreachable, exclusive clubs. The perfect example of this is without doubt the Augusta National in Georgia, which each year, in early April, hosts the prestigious Masters, which is the only one of the four Major Championships to be played always at the same course. On the extreme opposite of the spectrum we have public golf courses, which range from simple courses that can be played for a couple of dollars, to international (and incredibly expensive) golf meccas, such as the amazing Pebble Beach or the infamous Pinehurst No. 2, probably the hardest golf course in the world.

Canada, too, has embraced golf with a passion, and it certainly does not lack the space to create links in extraordinary natural settings. There are over 2000 courses in this vast North American country, many of which are worth taking the long trip to reach them. A superb example is Banff Springs, hidden in the forests of the Rocky Mountains at an altitude of about (4900 ft/1500 m). While in startling contrast to this mountainous course are the dazzling blue seas and sunny skies to be enjoyed playing the fairways of Bermuda, the Bahamas, and Hawaii. These vacation paradises are where golf is one of the most popular ways to relax.

222 left The rigorous beauty of Pinehurst.

222 center Banff Springs: a Canadian jewel.

222 right The magic of the ocean at Pebble Beach.

223 Augusta National, the garden of the Masters.

224-225 and 225 The Banff
Springs Golf Club is situated on
the valley floor along the Bow
River, beneath the peaks of
Sulphur Mountain and Mount
Roundle. We are in the heart of

Alberta, the vast province in
western Canada. A wild and
rugged landscape that has
contributed to making this
breathtakingly beautiful course
a true masterpiece.

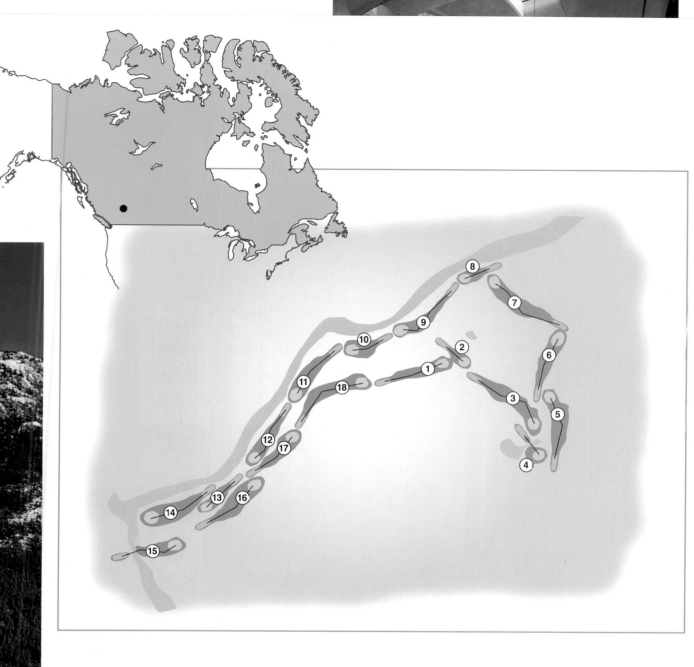

Banff Springs

ALBERTA (CANADA)

HOLE	1	2	3	4	5	6	7	8	9
YARDS	432	179	536	199	431	381	610	158	510
PAR	4	3	5	3	4	4	5	3	5

HOLE	10	11	12	13	14	15	16	17	18		TOT
YARDS	386	369	547	197	390	481	417	141	429		6793
PAR	4	4	5	3	4	5	4	3	4		72

Deep in the heart of the Canadian north is a course situated in the stunning wild landscape of the Rockies. It is impossible to forget its holes nestled in the pine forests and positioned in front of the imposing wall of rock that rises to the peaks of Sulphur Mountain and Mount Rundle, almost 9850 ft (3000 m) high. This is country you will remember for a lifetime, which poses one of the biggest challenges – trying to concentrate on golf while surrounded by this breathtaking scenery. At an international level, the 18 holes of the Banff Spring Golf Course deserve a place in the top ten of spectacular courses. And that is probably what the men of the Canadian Pacific Railway Company must have imagined when back in 1911 they chose the area enclosed within the huge Banff National Park to create a nine-hole course. It was intended to be one of the area's main attractions, along with a sensational towered hotel known as "the Castle in the Rockies." It immediately became a success and during the period of the First World War it was decided to build another nine holes according to Donald Ross's designs.

The big step up in the quality of the course's design occurred with the arrival of Stanley Thompson, the legendary Canadian golf architect. Stanley, who was of Scottish heritage, and his four brothers Nicol, Matt, Frank, and Bill became famous as the "Amazing Thompsons" for their great skill at designing courses. In the years 1921 to 1924 they literally dominated Canadian golf. A true legend of his time, Stanley, together with Donald Ross, founded the American Society of Golf Course Architects, and during his studies in Toronto and Guelph he became a mentor for talented young designers, especially the renowned Robert Trent Jones. Over 150 courses were created by Stanley Thompson between 1912 and 1953, but Banff Springs is probably his most famous work.

Banff Springs

228 and 228-229 The Fairmont Banff Springs course is one of the world's most spectacular mountain courses. At about 4900 ft (1500 m) above sea level it is open only

five months a year, from early May to early October. Its most beautiful hole is the 4th, a par 3 of 199 yards (182 m), where the ball has to clear the glacial lake.

229 bottom The 6793 yards (6211 m) of the Stanley Thompson Course in Banff Springs is a respectable length. Its incredible

location, in the deep north, makes life hard for the greenkeepers, who still manage miraculously to keep the course in perfect condition.

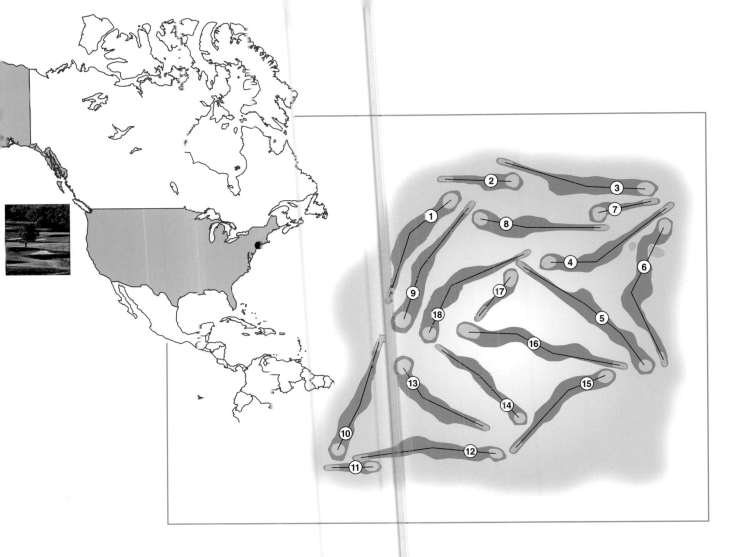

Shinnecock Hills

NEW YORK (USA)

HOLE	1	2	3	4	5	6	7	8	9			
YARDS	391	221	456	409	529	456	184	361	411			
PAR	4	3	4	4	5	4	3	4	4			

HOLE	10	11	12	13	14	15	16	17	18		TOT	
YARDS	412	158	469	372	447	400	542	169	426		6813	
PAR	4	3	4	4	4	4	5	3	4		70	

When in 1995 the centennial U.S. Open had to be organized, the U.S. Golf Association had to decide which course was the most representative to host such an important event. For a course to be able to bear such an honor and burden, it had to be significantly historical, it needed an elegant layout that was able to cope with the modern game, it needed to be well balanced yet tough, and also large enough to accommodate the huge crowds and accompanying amenities necessary for hosting such an event.

The choice fell on Shinnecock Hills, which offered a very hilly terrain, narrow fairways, impenetrable roughs, fast greens, 150 bunkers, the unpredictable wind, and a memorable clubhouse that overlooks everything from on high. As far as history is concerned, in 1894, Shinnecock Hills was a founder member, along with the Brookline Country Club, Newport Country Club in Rhode Island, the Chicago Golf Club, and St. Andrews in New York, of what would become the U.S. Golf Association. The course's history is certainly venerable and somewhat contentious as there are two versions. One history tells of a 12-hole course founded by a group of enthusiasts from Long Island who in 1890 got acquainted with golf and the Scottish pro Willie Dunn during a vacation in Biarritz, France. They were so enthralled by the game that they hired Dunn to build a course in Southampton, 1 mile (2 km) from the Atlantic on a treeless land that had links-style characteristics. The other version has it that after asking for assistance from the Royal Montreal Golf Club (the oldest in North America), Willie Davis, Royal Montreal's pro, was given a month's leave and sent to Southampton. Willie enlisted the help of 150 Shinnecock Native Americans from the nearby reservation. The 12-hole course was inaugurated in August 1891 and thus was born one of the first club in the States: a milestone that from the very beginning was the center of attention among American architects interested in studying this innovation.

The game got a foothold in the Hamptons and the increasing number of enthusiasts required the course to be expanded to 18 holes, which took place in 1895.

230 Tiger Woods in the 2004
U.S. Open at Shinnecock Hills,
which has hosted the U.S. Open
four times in three different
centuries: in 1896 (won by James
Foulis), 1986 (Ray Floyd), 1995
(Corey Pavin), and in 2004
(Retief Goosen).

230-231 and 231 bottom
The symbol of Shinnecock Hills,
the elegant clubhouse designed
by the architect Stanford White,
dominates the course from atop
a hill. The club has a glorious
past: in 1894, together with four
other clubs, it founded what
became the U.S. Golf
Association.

232-233, 232 bottom and 233
The origins of Shinnecock Hills
date back to 1891 with the 12
holes designed by the Scot Willie
Dunn, which were extended to
18 four years later. The course
was then redesigned by
Macdonald and Raynor and then
further remodeled in the early
1930s by Toomey & Flynn.
Narrow fairways, impenetrable
roughs, fast greens, and 150
bunkers are the characteristic
traits of this course, with the
wind as an added factor.

About 15 years later Macdonald and Raynor were consulted to touch up the course, but Shinnecock Hills' rise to fame was not their doing. In fact, in 1937, a highway development cut the course in two. The club had no choice but to purchase new land in the north and give up the portion south of the road. But every cloud has a silver lining, because it was a much better terrain for the new 18-hole course. The design of the new course was entrusted to Toomey and Flynn. Others associate this phase with the work of the 150 Native Americans on the course that was inaugurated in 1931 and that still today is the masterpiece of the two American architects. They relied on the land's vast size – 260 very lively acres (105

hectares), especially on the second part of the course – to create a masterly series of holes. These branch out in all directions, leaving the golfer with the difficult task of understanding where the wind is coming from on every hole. There are only two instances where two consecutive holes run in the same direction, the 2nd and the 3rd, and the 11th and the 12th. The wind itself is one of the deciding factors of the layout. The holes under the wind are longer and they open up at the end, while the ones above the wind are shorter and narrower. There are only two par 5s, which play in opposite directions, but the game can completely alter if the wind makes a 180-degree change of direction

234-235 Jim Furyk plays towards the green of the 18th hole at Oakmont with its distinctive clubhouse. The club is located near Pittsburgh, the second city of Pennsylvania, next to the Allegheny River. Despite its location there are no water hazards on the course.

234 bottom There are 210 bunkers at Oakmont, making it one of most difficult courses in North America.

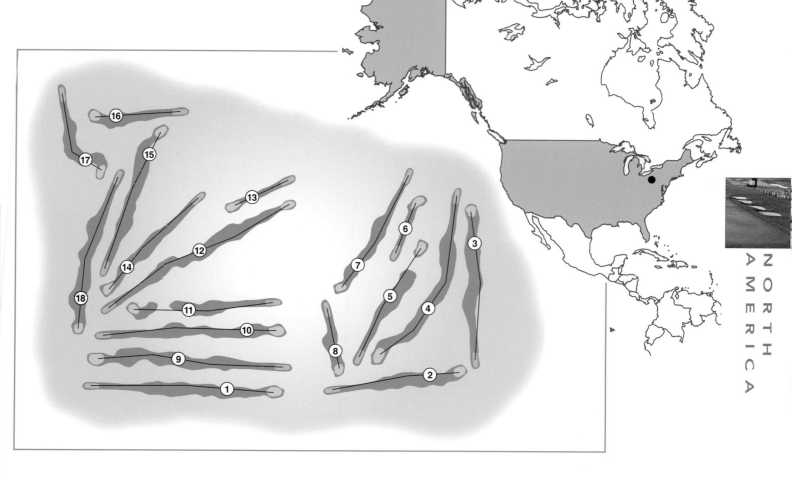

Oakmont

PENNSYLVANIA (USA)

HOLE	1	2	3	4	5	6	7	8	9
YARDS	482	340	428	609	382	194	479	288	477
PAR	4	4	4	5	4	3	4	3	5

HOLE	10	11	12	13	14	15	16	17	18		TOT
YARDS	462	379	667	183	358	499	231	313	484		7255
PAR	4	4	5	3	4	4	3	4	4		71

The Oakmont Country Club's immense reputation is beyond dispute. A long list of premier events have been held here and it is currently the club that has hosted the most U.S. national championships. The gorgeous Pennsylvania course also holds the record of eight U.S. Opens (1927, 1935, 1953, 1962, 1973, 1983, 1994, and 2007), along with three PGA Championships, the 1992 U.S. Women's Open, and five U.S. Amateurs.

Located in the suburbs northeast of Pittsburgh, the club is only a few yards away from the Allegheny, the Ohio River's main tributary. Even though it is close to a major river, the course has no water hazards on its 18 holes. Not even trees are a factor here, as one of the improvements of the course involved removing 4000 shrubs and trees. However, Oakmont is still considered by many to be the hardest course in North America, because it is rich with many other obstacles that are often difficult to clear. Even champions are nervous when they face its 210 bunkers, which are deep and perfectly placed along the course. A mention must be made of the most famous, the Church Pews (an obvious churchly reference) which comes into play on the 3rd and 4th holes. It is almost 330 ft (100 m) long and 130 ft (40 m) wide, with 12 grassy crests that interrupt the uniformity of the sand. A fearsome adversary (which comes in a smaller version on the 15th as well) that often changes the standings of the most important competitions.

Let us not forget also the enormous 390 ft (120 m) bunker named the "Sahara" defending the green of the extremely long 8th hole, a par 3 of 288 yards (262 m), or the "Big Mouth," a scary bunker to the right of the 17th green. The true nightmares of the course are the greens, however, which are proverbially fast and fiendishly undulating, combined with the hard terrain that will not stop even the most controlled approach. A tremendous challenge that can unsettle even champions and literally drive medium-level players crazy. The Oakmont Country Club was created in 1903 by Henry Clay Fownes.

235 Angel Cabrera walks along the 18th hole at Oakmont, where he won the 2007 U.S. Open. The Argentinean achieved an incredible score of a five shots below par, confirming that the course designed by Henry Clay Fownes in 1903 is still capable of making life hard for modern champions.

236 top *Even the phenomenal Tiger Woods managed to lose his cool during the 2007 U.S. Open on the tough Oakmont course. Of all the major courses, Oakmont has undergone the least modifications to its original design. The greens are unmodified, diabolical, and extremely fast, except for the 8th hole, which was moved to make space for the Pennsylvania Turnpike.*

236 bottom and 236-237 *The only blemish of the fabulous Oakmont course is that it is divided in two by Interstate 76, which separates the seven eastern holes, from the 2nd to the 8th holes, from the rest of the course. However, for the rest of the course there are only superlatives, starting with the incredible level of maintenance, despite the difficulties of maintaining 210 bunkers, which are mostly extremely complex.*

A steel magnate and an excellent golfer, though he only began playing the game at age 40 when he was introduced to it by another American steel tycoon, Andrew Carnegie. Carnegie, who went down in history as one of the richest man of all time, was born in Dunfermline, a few miles northwest of Edinburgh, Scotland. He emigrated to the United States at age 13, taking with him his passion for golf. Fownes took part in four U.S. Amateur competitions, the first of which was in 1901. Soon after, he devoted himself to planning Oakmont, which is the only course he designed. The construction was very fast. It began on the morning of 15th September 1903 with Fownes leading a crew of 150 men with two dozen mules. Twelve holes were built in only six weeks, then construction was halted due to the arrival of winter. The remaining six holes were finished in no time by the spring, and the course was opened for play in the summer of 1904.

Fownes' object of building the world's most challenging golf course was a success, and still is even after a century. It must be said that this Pittsburgh course has undergone the fewest improvements of all the major courses. It has maintained its greens intact, except for the one on the 8th hole, which was moved significantly to make space for the Pennsylvania Turnpike in the late 1940s. This is the only blemish on this course, which is divided in two by the highway that separates the seven eastern holes (from the 2nd to the 8th) from the rest of the course. When measured from the green tees, the furthest back, the infamous Oakmont course is 7255 yards (6632 m), but remarkably when an important championship is played it is a par 70!

Oakmont

237 bottom Oakmont's icon is the massive bunker known as the Church Pews, 330 ft (100 m) long and 130 ft (40 m) wide, between the 3rd and 4th holes with its 12 grassy "crests" interrupting the surface of the sand. Other famous bunkers include the Sahara, 390 ft (120 m) long and 100 ft (30 m) wide, and the infamous Big Mouth next to the green of the 17th.

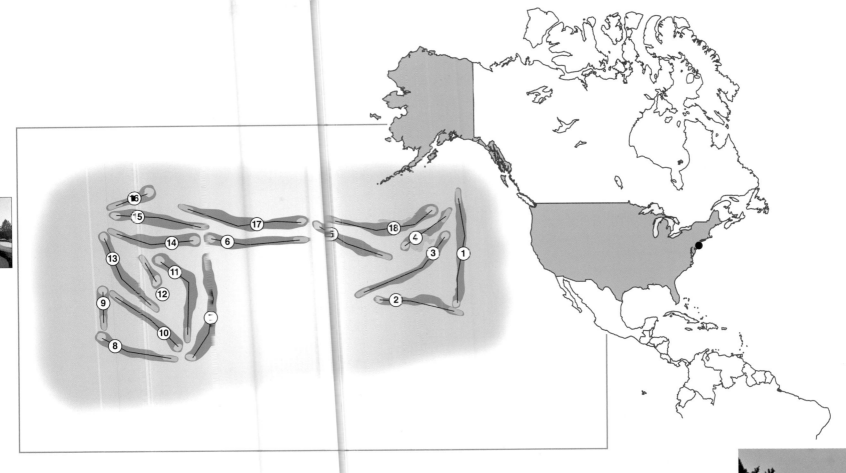

Baltusrol

NEW JERSEY (USA)

HOLE	1	2	3	4	5	6	7	8	9
YARDS	478	371	451	186	395	465	500	374	205
PAR	5	4	4	3	4	4	5	4	3

HOLE	10	11	12	13	14	15	16	17	18		TOT
YARDS	444	422	202	401	406	415	210	570	520		7015
PAR	4	4	3	4	4	4	3	5	5		72

Even in Manhattan you are not far from a world-class golf course. All you need to do is go through the Holland Tunnel, leaving Newark Airport behind, and just a few miles from the heart of the city you will reach Baltusrol, one of the most beautiful and exclusive clubs in the United States. The history of the club in Springfield Township, New Jersey, more or less mirrors the history of the game itself in America. In fact, its founding dates back to the last decade of the 19th century when Louis Keller, the editor of the *New York Social Register* (a directory of names and addresses of prominent citizens first published in 1886) was won over by golf, which was becoming increasingly popular. He therefore decided to create a course on the 495 acres (200 hectares) of land he had purchased near the Hudson River. The area formerly belonged to a certain

Baltus Roll, who was murdered in his house on 22nd February 1831. This was a notorious crime at the time, involving a long and detailed trial. Keller decided to name the club after its old landowner and announced its official opening on 19th October 1895. The first 30 members had nine well-designed holes to play based on a typical Scottish design.

Baltusrol's fame quickly spread thanks to its strategic position near New York and to affluent and socially prominent members. In only three years the number of club members reached 400, making Baltusrol a highly important meeting place in the social life of New York's upper class. In 1902, the club was chosen as the headquarters of the U.S. Women's Amateur Championship, an event that had originated only six years before at the Meadow Brook Club in Hempstead (NY). In 1903, it was the turn of the U.S. Open, won by William Law "Willie" Anderson, a Scottish immigrant who won the event four times. After that the American championship returned to Springfield another six times (1915, 1936, 1954, 1967, 1980, and 1993), where it was played on three different courses, a true record for this event. The year 1909 was another important period for the club, because a fire destroyed the clubhouse.

238 *Baltusrol has two 18-hole course, the Lower and the Upper. This is a club with a great tradition and a short distance from the center of New York.*

In the last few decades the Lower Course has been used to host major events, but Baltusrol holds the record for hosting the U.S. Open on three different courses.

238-239 *The big Baltusrol clubhouse dominates the 4th hole of the Lower Course, an insidious par 3 well defended by a water obstacle and about 186 yards (170 m) long. The club is in Springfield, New Jersey.*

239 top *Tiger Woods on the 18th of the Lower Course at Baltusrol during the 2005 PGA Championship, which was won by Phil Mickelson.*

Baltusrol

It was rebuilt much larger and more beautiful than before and three years later it officially hosted a U.S. president, William Howard Taft, which was a first for any golf club.

However, the original course started to feel too small for the club, which was still steadily growing. And so Albert Warren Tillinghast, one of the most accomplished and prolific golf architects (he designed over 250 courses, among them Bethpage, Medinah, and Winged Foot) was given the ambitious project of updating and improving the course. Tillinghast designed two amazing courses, the Upper and the Lower, which erased the original Baltusrol course and quickly became among the most highly regarded championship courses in the United States. The club survived the difficulties of the Great Depression in the 1930s and the disruption of the Second World War unscathed. In 1954, it was the host of a momentous event in the history of golf. In that year, the U.S. Open was broadcast on television, and millions were able to appreciate the Baltusrol course and watch Ed Furgol gain his incredible victory when he played the 18th of the Lower from the fairway of the Upper Course.

In 1952 the great Robert Trent Jones revisited the two Springfield courses, and in 1992 Rees Jones did the same. The most famous of the "twins" is the Lower Course, which for the last great competition held on it (the 2005 PGA Championship) measured 7015 yards (6414 m) and, as often happens during a Major, "lost" two strokes for a final par of 70. The three most beautiful holes are the 4th, the 17th, and the 18th. The first is a delicate par 3 of 185 yards (170 m) which forces players to hit the ball over a pond to a two-tiered green, while the others are two very difficult par 5s. An unusual yet extremely fascinating finish.

240 Baltusrol has a long tradition that dates back to the late 19th century when Louis Keller, publisher of the New York Social Register, decided to create a course on his estate on the shores of the Hudson. The area used to belong to a certain Baltus Roll, from which the club took its name.

240-241 The two courses at Baltusrol were designed by the great Albert Warren Tillinghast, one of the best golf architects of all time. Later, the Lower and the Upper courses were updated by Robert Trent Jones in 1952 and Rees Jones in 1992.

241 bottom The Lower Course is the championship course at Baltusrol and is among the longest and most challenging courses in the world. It measures 7015 yards (6414 m) and has a par of 70 shots instead of the traditional 72. The most beautiful holes are considered to be the 4th, the 17th, and the 18th.

Baltusrol

242-243 Davis Love III faces the difficult bunkers of the 18th on the Lower at Baltusrol. In the long and rich history of the club, some memorable years include 1909 (the clubhouse fire), 1912 (William President Howard Taft's visit, the first official golf visit for a U.S. president), and 1954 (firt television broadcast of the Open).

243 Baltusrol has hosted the U.S. Open seven times. The first time it was held here was in 1903, when it was won by William Law "Willie" Anderson, a Scottish immigrant who won this prestigious competition four times.

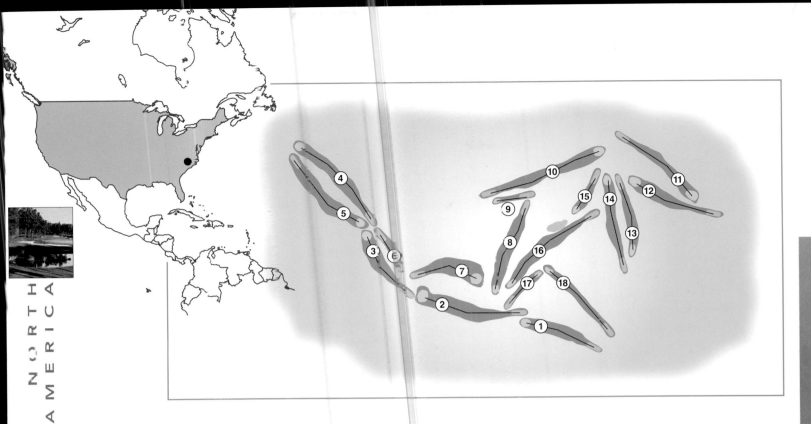

Pinehurst

NORTH CAROLINA (USA)

HOLE	1	2	3	4	5	6	7	8	9
YARDS	391	432	327	503	442	194	397	487	165
PAR	4	4	4	5	4	3	4	5	3

HOLE	10	11	12	13	14	15	16	17	18		TOT
YARDS	569	427	368	365	417	183	492	165	417		6741
PAR	5	4	4	4	4	3	5	3	4		72

Behind the story of Pinehurst is the Bostonian magnate James Walker Tufts. In 1875 he sold his Soda Fountain Company for $700,000, but dissatisfied with his retirement at 60 he decided to reinvest his money philanthropically. He was a man of great initiative but poor health. He wanted to create a resort in the central-south area for those who wanted refuge from the fierce New England winters and for people with tuberculosis who needed a mild climate. He had heard about the healing properties of the Sandhills in North Carolina, so he purchased 5500 acres (2225 hectares) where he built a hotel, vacation homes, some motels, recreation areas, pinic areas, and so forth. The amount of land available (initially called "Tuftstown" by the locals then named Pinehurst) meant that almost anything could be hosted here.

In 1897, Tufts saw a group of guests hitting small balls on the fields with some wooden clubs. He was very interested and discovered that they were playing golf. He had at once had nine holes built and it was an immediate success, so he doubled the number and in December 1900 he even employed a golf coach, a Scottish immigrant called Donald Ross. Ross designed an additional nine holes that became 18 in 1907 and thus the Pinehurst No. 2 course was created. By 1923 there were two more courses, also created by Ross.

244 The Pinehurst resort was created with the philantropic aim of providing New Englanders with a healthy retreat from the rigors of winter.

244-245 The logo of Pinehurst is the "Putter Boy," a 1912 statue that was designed to act as a sundial with his shaft. It is said that Donald Ross himself posed to show the exact stance and grip. The statue was later moved in the area of the putting green.

245 bottom East of the clubhouse there are the bronze statues of Donald Ross (left) and Richard Tufts, who for years was the director and then vice-president of the Southern Golf Association. The Pinehurst clubhouse is one of the world's most famous. Built in 1898, when the first 18 holes were completed, it was renovated in 1901 with the addition of a second floor. In 1922 it underwent its most significant modifications, taking on its present-day appearance.

Pinehurst

246-247 Of the last four holes at Pinehurst No. 2, two are tough par 3s. The 15th hole is 183 yards (167 m) long from the back tees and presents one of the most problematic greens. It is unlikely for the ball to remain on the green with a tee shot: short shots roll back and the deep bunkers are ready to swallow any shots that go right.

247 top The 5th hole is probably the hardest par 4 in America. It is 442 yards (404 m) long and made life miserable for many players in the 1999 U.S. Open, forcing players to take an average of 4.55 shots to complete it. Along with the 4th hole, it was added to the course in 1935.

In no other place in the United States was golf such an extensive part of the landscape and it was destined to become even more so and since 1996 Pinehurst now has eight courses (a number exceeded in 2004 by the 12 courses at Mission Hills, China).

Of the eight courses, the No. 2 is the longest at 6741 yards (6163 m) from the championship tees. It is beautiful, world famous, tough, and has hosted the most important U.S. tournaments, such as the 1999 and 2005 U.S. Opens (it will host it again in 2014). It is not so much the length that is intimidating, but rather the fastest greens in the world, each with many slopes leading the ball away from the hole and from the green itself. If power is recommended, then a short precise game is essential to play this course, as well as a caddie, at least for the first time. What is also intimidating is the very irregular terrain, the water hazards, the well-placed bunkers, and the overall layout which all test players whatever their ability. "The most balanced test for championship golf" as Ross himself defined it, or "The American St. Andrews," as it was renamed by Bobby Jones, or as Tiger Woods said: "Pure golf fun." In other words golf as it was meant to be played, which can make you laugh with joy or cry in despair. More powerful players, more technologically advanced clubs, and longer-flying golf balls still have not managed to crack Ross's work.

The course stretches out into broad corridors of pines with fairways wide enough to allow players to aim right or left, according to the flag's position. Its greens are essentially its forte. They are on average 610 sq yards (510 sq m) wide, half of this area is unusable for the flag due to the inclinations and slopes. All you need is a misdirected short chip and the ball will roll back and you will have to start over again. It may not have the grandeur of a Cypress Point, but Pinehurst No. 2 is rightfully famous for its greens alone. Particular mention must be made of the 5th, a par 4 of 442 yards (404 m) that is probably the toughest green in American golf. It was definitely the toughest one in the 1999 U.S. Open when players took an average of 4.55 shots to close it out. It has a very difficult approach requiring a long iron and with the ball higher than the player's feet. If you approach from the left you risk a frustrating up-and-down. Once you are on the green, you need to evaluate its bewildering inclinations, which is a challenge even for pros with their caddies.

247 center The body of water in front of the tee of the 16th is the only lake on this course and does not come into play. For those who play regularly, this hole is a par 5, but for the 1999 U.S. Open it was turned into a par 4.

247 bottom The 7th is the par 4 that presents the most accentuated dogleg of the course. A handful of bunkers are ready to welcome any drives that head off to the right. Powerful players can try to cut the elbow to approach the green.

248-249 The 4th holes is the first par 5 of the course and provides a birdie opportunity, as long you keep to the fairway and get to the green in two shots, paying close attention to the large bunker on the left. Otherwise you can hit the first

shot into the middle of the bunker about 87 yards (80 m) from the green and face the approach with a short iron.

249 top If the bunker on the 16th fairway is not a big problem, the two bunkers

guarding the green on the right certainly are.

249 center The 10th is a par 5 and the longest of the course. The more powerful players can reach the green in two shots, avoiding the bunker on the left.

249 bottom The 8th is normally a par 5 but becomes a par 4 for the U.S. Open Championship. The crucial shot at this hole is the approach to the green, which slopes from back to front.

Pinehurst

250-251 and 251 The Augusta National Golf Club is the only course to be the permanent venue of one of the four Majors, the Masters, which every year takes place here during the first "complete" week of April. Bobby Jones's 18 holes can only be visited during big events, as it is a private club with very strict rules about access.

250 bottom An army of greenkeepers at Augusta is busy making the course perfect for the Masters held in early April.

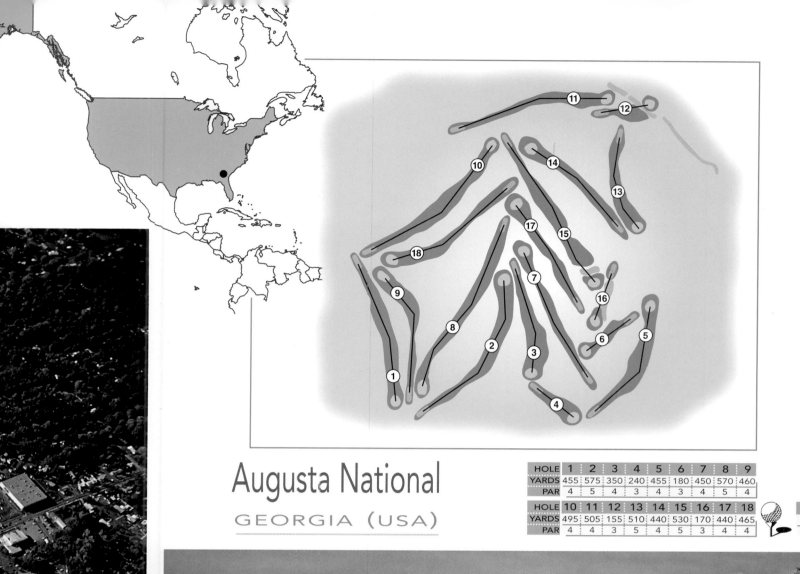

Augusta National
GEORGIA (USA)

HOLE	1	2	3	4	5	6	7	8	9
YARDS	455	575	350	240	455	180	450	570	460
PAR	4	5	4	3	4	3	4	5	4

HOLE	10	11	12	13	14	15	16	17	18		TOT
YARDS	495	505	155	510	440	530	170	440	465		7445
PAR	4	4	3	5	4	5	3	4	4		72

There is something magical about Augusta National. The course that was founded by the great Bobby Jones and is the only one in the world to have hosted one of the four Majors, the Grand Slam tournaments, every year. This phenomenal record gives it an extraordinary aura, comparable to the great St. Andrews.

Golf's elite gather at Augusta, the Georgia city right on the border with South Carolina, during the first "complete" week of April (a tradition that began in 1940) to start the only tournament that can rival the British Open Championship. Robert Tyre Jones Jr., aka "Bobby," the legendary champion of the 1920s from Georgia, designed Augusta with Clifford Roberts and the British architect Alistair MacKenzie for the specific purpose of hosting an international tournament, starting in 1934. From the beginning Roberts decided to call it "The Masters Tournament," but Jones considered it to be too presumptuous and decided to fall back on the more humble "Augusta National Invitation Tournament," which was the title used until 1939 when Bobby gave in to his friends' pressure.

The Masters is an icon of America's golf tradition and it was responsible for developing many standards that have been adopted by all the most important tournaments. For instance, its 72 holes, played in four consecutive days, from Thursday to Sunday, as well as the cancellation of qualification rounds, and the introduction of the rule that allows only players and their caddies to be in the playing area. All the names of the great champions are recorded in the annals of the Masters, from Sarazen to Snead

252-253 The 13th, the last of the
famous "Amen Corner" trio, is
among the most beautiful and
challenging hole on the Augusta
course. It is called the "Azalea"
due to the gorgeous azaleas that
surround the green.

252 bottom One of the
characteristics of Augusta is the
presence of water hazards, an
example is the small lake located
next to the 16th hole.

253 top After having brought the
tees back 54 yards (50 m) in 2002,
the 18th hole went back to being
a respectable adversary, worthy of
a masterpiece like the Augusta
National.

253 bottom Every hole at Augusta
bears the name of the most visible
flowers on the course: Tea Olive,
Dogwood, Flowering Peach,
Flowering Crabapple, Magnolia,
Juniper, Pampas, Yellow Jasmine,
Carolina Cherry, Camellia, White
Dogwood, Golden Bell, Azalea,
Chinese Fir, Fire Thorn, Redbud,
Nandina, and Holly.

and Nelson, from Hogan to Palmer, Nicklaus (he has the record of six victories), Falco, Ballesteros, Watson, and, naturally, Tiger Woods, who in 1997, only 21 years and three months old, established the new record on 72 holes of 270 strokes, which had been unchallenged for 32 years. Equally famous is the "green jacket," the official uniform for club members, which is awarded to the winner and is presented by the previous year's winner. The champion may keep it for a year, he will then have to give it back and can only use it within the club, of which every Masters winner is automatically made an honorary member. The large silver trophy, a reproduction of the clubhouse, is also an important part of the Master tradition. The superb course of Augusta is the crown jewel of one of the most exclusive clubs in the world. There are about 300 members, who are admitted only by invitation and who pay an annual fee of thousands of dollars. Woman can play as guests, but cannot become members.

The 18 holes at Augusta are closed from June to October, and are famous all over the world for their extraordinary botanical beauty. Each hole carries the name of a plant or shrub to which it is associated, such as the Magnolia (5th hole), the Camellia (10th), and the Azalea (13th). The decision to hold the Masters in the first half of April is certainly not accidental, because this is the period when the flowers along the course are at their most spectacular best. It is really difficult to choose the most beautiful holes, so we will focus on the most famous ones, those that comprise the famous "Amen Corner" – the 11th, the 12th, and the 13th. The trio were named the "Amen Corner" in 1958 by the journalist Herbert Warren Wind writing in *Sports Illustrated*. The name derives from an old jazz tune, "Shouting at Amen Corner," and it underlines the critical importance of the three holes: a par 4 of 505 yards (about 460 m), the "White Dogwood," followed by the "Golden Bell," a par 3 and probably the most beautiful and infamous hole in the world, and the superlative and extremely difficult "Azalea," a par 5 of 510 yards (466 m). The three holes are linked by the presence of Rae's Creek, a sinuous water obstacle in which many dreams of victory have drowned. The 18th hole, "Holly," is also beautiful and has a prohibitive tee shot down a long, very narrow corridor of trees, followed by the large amphitheatre that hosts the often dramatic events of the Masters finale. Let us not forget the famous little bridges of Augusta, dedicated to the two golf champions and Masters winners, Byron Nelson (first in 1937 and 1942) and Gene Sarazen (1935).

Among the many anecdotes associated with the course, mention must be made of the one involving President Eisenhower, to whom a pine tree on the 17th is dedicated, a tree which he hit so many times he officially requested for it to be removed. The pro-

Augusta National

posal was never fulfilled, but as a consolation, Ike's Pond, a beautiful pond, was created upon the advice of the president.

The feeling when entering the clubhouse is truly remarkable. It is a continually evolving "museum" of world golf. On the first floor we encounter the Grill Room (its hamburgers and its peach cobbler are renowned) and the Trophy Room, where, when the Masters is over, the gala dinnper for club members is held with the winner as the guest of honor. But the most famous room is the Champions Locker Room, dedicated to the winners of the Masters: there are 28 lockers marked with brass plates bearing the names of the champions. On the upper floor we have the Crow's Nest, a room with a large glass cupola and five beds, reserved for the amateurs who each year are invited to play the Masters.

254 top The bridges over Raes Creek are dedicated to the champions of golf, such as the Hogan Bridge on the 12th hole, the Nelson Bridge on the 13th, and the Sarazen Bridge on the 15th.

254 center The bunkers at Augusta are often large, carved out with great patience, and extremely challenging. Classic example are the ones next to the greens of the 4th, 12th, and 16th holes, all charming par 3s that have witnessed many historic moments.

Augusta National

254 bottom Robert Tyre Jones Jr., aka Bobby, designed the Augusta in the early 1930s along with Clifford Roberts and Alister MacKenzie from England. From 1934 this course has been the setting for the crowning of many of the great golf champions, from Sarazen to Snead, Hogan to Palmer, Nicklaus to Faldo, Ballesteros, Watson, and Tiger Woods.

254-255 Exiting the bunker on the gorgeous "Golden bell" par 3, the second hole of the Amen Corner. The winner of the Master gets the famous green jacket, which is presented by the winner from the previous year. The champion may keep the jacket for a year, he will then have to give it back and can only wear it within the club grounds.

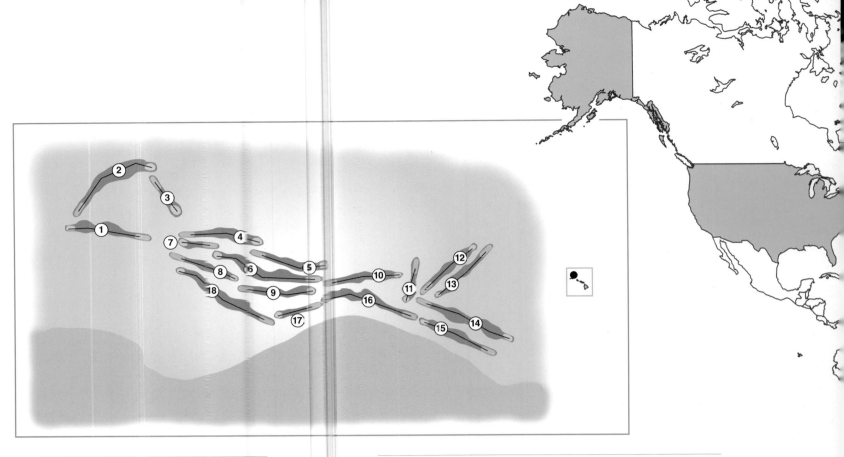

HOLE	1	2	3	4	5	6	7	8	9
YARDS	428	524	209	380	355	573	52	334	405
PAR	4	5	3	4	4	5	3	4	4

HOLE	10	11	12	13	14	15	16	17	18		TOT
YARDS	394	193	412	384	537	427	01	201	550		6959
PAR	4	3	4	4	5	4	4	3	5		72

Poipu Bay

HAWAII (USA)

256 and 257 Inaugurated in 1991, from 1994 to 2006 Poipu Bay was the venue for the PGA Grand Slam of Golf, one of the most prestigious tournaments that features 36 holes and only the winners of the four Majors (Masters, U.S. Open, Open Championship, and PGA Championship) can compete for a total prize of over 1 million dollars. Tiger Woods won it five years straight, from 1998 to 2002, establishing a tournament record.

Aloha! A great big smile (but no lay), golf carts with GPS systems to help players better their score on an unknown course, and, at the end of the day, a fresh lemon-scented towelette: this is how you are welcomed at Poipu Bay, the course designed by Robert Trent Jones Jr. in Kaua on a rolling plateau about 100 ft (30 m) from the Pacific. On one side are the lush mountains so typical of Hawaii, while on the other is the ocean rich with whales, monk seals, and sea turtles. In the distance is the surprising rock formation known as Mahualepu, which legend has it is a completely submerged Hawaiian god, with only the tip of his nose emerging from the water. The course features an old stone wall and the remains of a *heiau*, a temple, which are said to radiate great spiritual power. Golfers are not allowed in these protected areas, so avoid hitting your ball here because you would not be able to play it and you would incur a penalty.

Inaugurated in 1991, Poipu Bay has from 1994 to 2006 hosted the PGA Grand Slam of Golf, which only the winners of the four Majors (Masters, U.S. Open, Open Championship, and PGA Championship) can play. The tournament is played over 36 holes for a grand prize of over one million dollars.

Poipu Bay

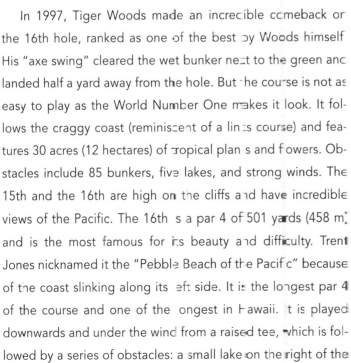

In 1997, Tiger Woods made an incredible comeback on the 16th hole, ranked as one of the best by Woods himself. His "axe swing" cleared the wet bunker next to the green and landed half a yard away from the hole. But the course is not as easy to play as the World Number One makes it look. It follows the craggy coast (reminiscent of a links course) and features 30 acres (12 hectares) of tropical plants and flowers. Obstacles include 85 bunkers, five lakes, and strong winds. The 15th and the 16th are high on the cliffs and have incredible views of the Pacific. The 16th is a par 4 of 501 yards (458 m) and is the most famous for its beauty and difficulty. Trent Jones nicknamed it the "Pebble Beach of the Pacific" because of the coast slinking along its left side. It is the longest par 4 of the course and one of the longest in Hawaii. It is played downwards and under the wind from a raised tee, which is followed by a series of obstacles: a small lake on the right of the fairway followed by two bunkers, a coastal cliff on the left, and a dogleg created by a *heiau* (which counts as an obstacle). The fairway and the green slope towards the ocean and more adventurous players can try to fly the ball along the coast and make it in two shots (maybe), or it can be safely played on the right and finished in par (maybe). The hardest of all is the 9th, a par 4 of 405 yards (370 m), well-protected by the trade wind as well as by the large bunkers on both sides of the fairway, which at a certain point narrows down to 24 yards (22 m). The second shot is played against the wind, with a single bunker defending the right side of the raised green. The green's usable surface is smaller than one would think due to the rather steep inclination. It is also the first hole to feature one of the four archeological sites scattered along the course and it includes a *heiau* made of lava rock, right of the fairway, which makes the game harder and more interesting.

259 bottom right The course features old stone walls and the remains of a heiau, an Hawaiian temple over 500 years old. These temples are said to radiate a great spiritual power, *but must be avoided. Golfers are not allowed in these protected areas, which are designated as hazards, so make sure you do not hit your ball here as you would nt be able to play it.*

258, 258-259 and 259 bottom left This Hawaiian course was designed by Robert Trent Jones Jr. in Kauai on a rolling plateau about 32 yards (30 m) from the Pacific. The stunning backdrop to this course is composed of *mountains and the ocean. The best views are probably from the 15th and 16th holes, the latter nicknamed by Trent Jones "the Pebble Beach of the Pacific" because it has the coast along its entire left side.*

Pebble Beach

264 top The wind and the ocean are not the only adversaries to face on the marvelous 18 holes of Pebble Beach, because the bunkers are large and cunningly sited.

264 bottom and 264-265 The 17th and 18th holes make the most fascinating of endings to a round of golf. The 18th especially allows spectators to see it in all

its beauty. It is a par 5 of 542 yards (495 meters) with a breathtaking out of bounds on the whole left side – the Pacific Ocean.

HOLE	1	2	3	4	5	6	7	8	9		TOT
YARDS	418	471	190	330	433	360	164	349	405		
PAR	4	5	3	4	4	4	3	4	4		

HOLE	10	11	12	13	14	15	16	17	18		TOT
YARDS	404	487	437	238	357	504	376	203	421		6548
PAR	4	5	4	3	4	5	4	3	4		71

270 Designed in the 1920s by the American Charles Blair MacDonald, the course was restructured in the early 1950s by Robert Trent Jones, *who fully respected the original design, which was proof of the esteem he had for the work of his predecessor.*

Mid Ocean

BERMUDA

The gentle, slightly rolling landscape of Bermuda, where the highest peak barely reaches 260 ft (80 m), makes the island look like one big golf course. The architects who designed the island's courses simply had to follow the lay of the land, without moving too much soil, to obtain varied and perfect layouts, so creating great games of golf and great landscapes. The most famous course in Bermuda is the Mid Ocean, a piece of Old England in Tucker's Town, on the northeastern tip of the island. It is expensive and exclusive, so much so that in order to gain entry you need to be introduced by a member (nonetheless, because some members are hotel owners, they can allow a limited number of guests to play on Monday, Wednesday, and Friday mornings). In other words, this is a VIP course and some of the people who have walked its fairways include Winston Churchill and former U.S. presidents Dwight Eisenhower, George Bush Snr., and Jimmy Carter.

Mid Ocean has always been on the list of the world's best courses and is a classic course that rewards good shots and punishes bad ones. It was designed by the American architect Charles Blair MacDonald, who was waiting for the right opportunity to express himself outside the United States with one of his legendary layouts. They found the necessary acres in 1919 and it was December two years later before the course was completed. Blair described it as one of his most important projects, praising its "beauty, its charm, and the quality of its links." He added: "I can assure my golfing fiends, a more fascinating, more picturesque course than the Mid-Ocean will not be found in a pilgrimage around the world.

270-271 The 12th hole is the most challenging par 4 of the course. The tee shot must clear the bunker on the right. A downwards slope in front of the green risks rolling the ball backwards on short approaches.

271 bottom Mark Twain, the master of aphorisms, said of Bermuda: "It is the biggest small place in the world," and that describes the place perfectly. However, if he had seen Mid Ocean, he probably would not have said that "Golf is a good walk spoiled." Bermuda is also the island with the highest concentration of golf courses per square mile, as well as banks.

272-273 The first three holes run parallel to the Atlantic Ocean, which does not come into play at all. The most famous of the 18 is the 5th hole, a par 4 with a tee raised above the water of a small lake, which has claimed famous victims such as the legendary baseball player Babe Ruth.

Mid Ocean

There is nothing commonplace about it." The shaky postwar economy affected the course, which was refurbished in the early 1950s by Robert Trent Jones, who did not leave a clearly visible mark of his presence, which was a sure sign of his respect for MacDonald's original design. After all, MacDonald was one of the driving forces of golf in the United States. Besides being the founder of the USGA and winner of the first official U.S. Amateur Championship, he invented the term "golf architect" and was the first to bear that title.

Mid Ocean is considered the most fascinating and picturesque course ever to be designed by an ocean, with the first three holes running parallel to the water, which never comes into play. It is also a tough course and you will probably need the views of the Atlantic to forget all those double and triple bogeys. The most famous hole is definitely the 5th, a par 4 of 433 yards (396 m) with a raised tee over an expanse of water, Mangrove Lake, which makes the fairway look further than it is in reality. It is into this lake that one afternoon the legendary baseball player Babe Ruth (1895–1948) lost a dozen balls in the pointless attempt of reaching the green. The green is protected by a sheer embankment that leads to

272 bottom The Mid Ocean is an exclusive club, some hotel owners are allowed to let a limited number of guests play here three days a week. The VIPs that have walked its fairways include Winston Churchill, Ike Eisenhower, George Bush, and Jimmy Carter.

273 The 13th hole is the longest par 3 in Bermuda (238 yards/218 m). It requires a long iron or a hybrid to reach the green, which is protected on the right and left by rows of trees and is slightly sloped from front to back.

the two bunkers, with a steep slope on the right that bounces the balls to the center of the green. If the 5th hole is included among the world's best par 4s, then the 1st is one of the most challenging opening holes in Bermuda. A par 4 of 418 yards (382 m), it doglegs to the left, requiring a tee shot from the right to left onto a fairway flanked by bunkers. While the 3rd hole is one of the most picturesque par 3s on the island, even though the starting position has been pulled back 14 yards (13 m) to make the tee shot more challenging. An accurate evaluation of the wind is required if you are going to choose the right club.

CENTRAL AND SOUTH AMERICA

The opportunities for golf to develop in Central and South America are enormous to say the least. At present there are less than a thousand courses and no more then 200,000 golfers, which are insignificant figures in comparison to those of the United States. Argentina and Brazil are the two main golf nations in South America, with 45,000 and 23,000 golfers respectively. While in the rest of the continent there are about 50 courses, mainly in Chile and Colombia.

There are very few golf courses in Bolivia, Paraguay, Peru, Uruguay, and Venezuela, where golf is a sport played by few. However, slowly but steadily golf is growing and developing, usually as part of tourism developments in the Caribbean, Mexico, and increasingly Brazil, which are designed to attract thousands of U.S. and Canadian golfers.

Golf arrived in Argentina after 1879. It was brought by the British entrepreneurs and engineers who came here to work and establish new businesses, usually related to the construction of the railroads. The first golf clubs in Argentina and Brazil were closely associated with the construction of the railroad network. The first regular Argentinean competition dates back to 1892, whereas only at the end of the century did Brazil follow suit, once again helped by the burgeoning rail system. Some British engineers, busy with over-seeing the São Paulo Railway, managed to convince the Benedictine monks to give up part of the land belonging to the São Bento monastery, where they built the first holes on Brazilian soil. Mexico's golf history is similar. Although in recent years it has been its closeness to the United States that has stimulated the investment in golf courses and resorts.

Magnificent resorts have been created both on the Atlantic and the Pacific coasts, where new agronomic technologies have enabled the creation of superb courses, even in Baja California, the long, narrow peninsula on the west coast. Despite the desert climate that only allows cactuses to grow in the infernal temperatures, there are many lush green courses scattered here and there between the U.S. border and the resorts around Cabo San Lucas, its southern tip.

The Caribbean offers paradise locations and through ingenious designs beautiful golf courses have been built on all of the sufficiently sized islands. The great tourist appeal of golf has resulted in the development of resorts from Jamaica to the Caymans, from Barbados to the Dominican Republic. These last two islands are the ones where golf has caught on the most. The British presence in Barbados meant that golf has long been an established pastime and so the island has been swift to encourage large golf resorts with villas and hotels.

274 left The gorgeous cliffs on which Casa de Campo stands.

274 center Golf in Cartagena offers players breathtaking views.

274 right The course of Cabo del Sol unfolds between the ocean coast and the desert.

275 The Gávea Golf & Country Club is one of the two courses in Rio de Janeiro.

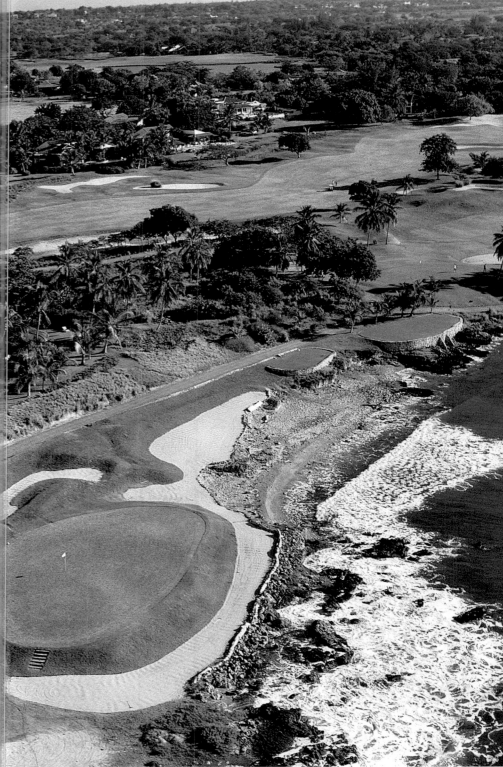

280-281 Teeth of the Dog is the local name of the pointy coral reef on which the course is built. This masterpiece of the Dominican Republic is the work of Pete Dye, who created another two courses at Casa de Campo (the Links and Dye Fore), with the help of his wife Alice, also an architect.

280 bottom Dead calm, no problem, but if the wind lifts then the "dog" shows its teeth and the ocean foam makes it seem "rabid."

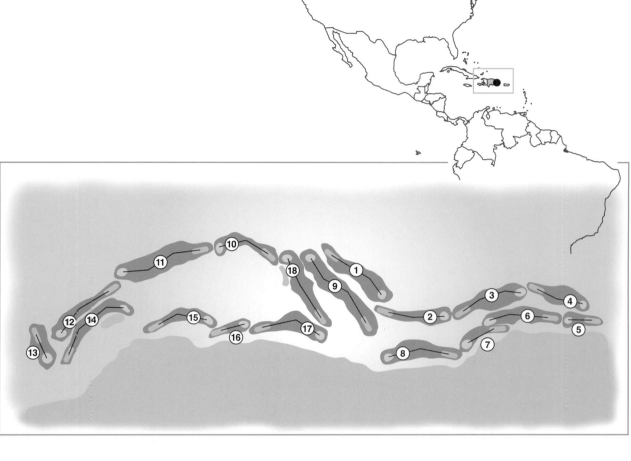

Casa de Campo

DOMINICAN REPUBLIC

HOLE	1	2	3	4	5	6	7	8	9
YARDS	401	378	545	327	155	449	225	417	505
PAR	4	4	5	4	3	4	3	4	5

HOLE	10	11	12	13	14	15	16	17	18		TOT
YARDS	377	540	445	175	505	384	185	435	440		6888
PAR	4	5	4	3	5	4	3	4	4		72

Casa de Campo is home to numerous sports, such as all those relating to water, naturally, since we are on a Caribbean island, plus horse-riding, polo, tennis, and target shooting. But the dominant sport is golf thanks to the three courses designed by Pete Dye, of which the Teeth of the Dog has been permanently in the top 100 best golf courses in the world since its inauguration in 1971. Dye took two years to build this course, with the help of his wife Alice (also an architect) and 300 local workers, who worked with machetes to clear the thick vegetation from the craggy coral coastline and to cover it with a mix of soils in order it makes the grass take. "Teeth of the dog" is actually the local name of the reef – notoriously sharp – on which the course was built. When the wind rages and you are sprayed by the ocean foam, you are actually reminded of a rabid dog.

The course follows a figure-of-eight shape, going clockwise out and vice versa on the way back in. The first four holes play inland and are characterized by large waste areas (sandy areas) that penetrate into the fairway, while deep bunkers protect the fast, raised greens. All three features are characteristic of Dye's design. The 5th to 8th holes follow the ocean, while the 9th to the 14th holes return back in to follow the water from the 15th to the 17th (you can enjoy a spectacular ocean sunset if you are looking for an excuse to play in the afternoon), only to leave it again on the last hole. There are two considerations to make when playing: first, the continuous changes in route involve a different wind direction from hole to hole; second, there are seven holes on the coast and even water, besides offering splendid views, influences the game. Dye, who acknowledges that this is his favorite course, is ready to admit that he only built 11 holes, while God created the remaining seven by the ocean.

Although it is a masterpiece, the course has been affected by the passing of time and the technological advances of the modern game.

281 The course was hand-built with the help of 300 workers who worked with machetes to clear the thick brush first and then used pickaxes and so forth to break the rock. The original terrain was replaced with a mix of different components – sand, soil, and organic residues from sugar refining – ideal for planting Bermuda grass.

Casa de Campo

So nearly 35 years after its creation it underwent a facelift that, besides redoing the starting tee, the green and the bunkers, lengthened the course by 470 yards (430 m) from the back tees. There are four par 3s, which are always the most fascinating and often most dangerous holes, three of which are played along the coast. The first one is the 5th hole, with a peninsula green that looks even smaller than it is because of the often sideways-blowing wind. There is a small landing area on the right, but you can easily hit the bunker and come out too long with the risk of landing in water. Before the modernization the hole was even more difficult, with a large tree on the right, in front of the green, which was torn down by a hurricane, much to the joy of golfers. (It pre-

vented them from attacking it from this side.) The second par 3 is the 7th, a long hole with many obstacles that are ready to catch any errant shots. The rather wide green is multi-leveled, so that even if you reach it, it isn't always easy to make the hole in two putts. The last par 3 on the water is the 16th, probably the most difficult of the trio, situated on a rocky bay modeled into some sort of a jaw that looks like it is ready to bite. It is also rather long (193 yards/177 m) and is against the wind, with a tree-lined green. The choice of clubs is not easy, especially when the wind whirls among the trees. It is even more difficult if the flag is on the right of the green, over the coral wall. To make up for any disappointing shots, just enjoy the fabulous view.

282 top left The ocean plays a fundamental role on the course, inaugurated in 1971, and seven of the holes follow the coast.

282 top right The layout is not a typical out and back, instead it follows a figure of eight shape. The first four holes are played on the inside and are characterized by barren sandy areas that are

wide but not deep. The bunkers – which are indeed deep – guard the greens.

282 bottom Almost 35 years after its creation, the course was revamped. The starting tees, the greens, and the bunkers have been modified, and it was also extended by 470 yards (430 m), from the back tees. The increase

in length effects the first nine holes especially.

283 Dye himself confesses that Teeth of the Dog is his favorite work, but he is ready to admit that it was designed by "the man up there". "I created eleven holes and God creates seven". The seven holes which he refers to are naturally the ones along the ocean.

284-285 Colin Montgomerie on a tee at Sandy Lane. There are 45 holes for those golfers lucky enough to play at Sandy Lane, a luxury resort on the island of Barbados, the easternmost island of the Caribbean.

284 bottom and 285 This internationally renowned resort is rightfully famous for its sumptuous and well-appointed rooms, as well as magnificent pools and spas.

Sandy Lane

BARBADOS

HOLE	1	2	3	4	5	6	7	8	9
YARDS	378	370	423	167	435	514	355	198	635
PAR	4	4	4	3	4	5	4	3	5

HOLE	10	11	12	13	14	15	16	17	18		TOT
YARDS	478	270	594	250	564	533	226	523	472		6755
PAR	4	3	5	3	5	5	3	4	4		72

Barbados is the easternmost island of the Caribbean, and in many ways it has its own, separate history. It has a higher standard of living compared to other Caribbean islands, just behind that of Canada and the United States. Barbados, in other words, is a happy island that derives its name from the "beard" growing on the fig tree (banyan) or on the American Indians met by the first Europeans. It was a British colony from 1627 to 1966, the year of its independence, and it is probably because of the British influence that it is one of the Caribbean countries with the most golf courses. There are five clubs with a total of seven courses, all concentrated on the west coast, which allow golfers to choose from all sorts of options for a high-class golf vacation. Barbados also enjoys all the perks of a moderate tropical climate, but is fortunately located on the edge of the hurricane zone. During the rainy season, which is from June to November, only once in 30 years have the biggest storms reached its coasts. The capital is Bridgetown and the island is divided into 11 parishes (rather than counties, provinces, or states). Apart from the parish of Christ Church, all of them are dedicated to saints. St. James' Parish is home to two of the island's most beautiful golf clubs, the Royal Westmoreland and Sandy Lane. The former boasts a superb course with 18 holes designed by Robert Trent Jones Jr., set in a country club of over 495 acres (200 hectares), dotted with prestigious villas. The Sandy Lane club is part of one of the world's most famous resorts.

Since 1961 Sandy Lane has provided five-star luxury in an exclusive environment, attracting film stars, singers, crowned

heads, and tycoons from all over the world. It is a gorgeous resort, facing a white coral beach, stretching for about 247 acres (100 hectares) among mahogany trees, gentle hills, and by a sea that ranges from sapphire to cobalt blue. The resort has 112 rooms and suites with every imaginable comfort and high-tech equipment discreetly hidden by an ultra-classic décor. The Spa, located in a Roman-style building is one of the best in the wellness and body treatment business. Lucky golfing guests at Sandy Lane also have 45 holes at their disposal, which make this resort a true golf paradise. In the middle of the course is a modern and very spacious clubhouse of over 54,000 sq ft (5000 sq m), which dominates the course. The first nine holes, the famous "Old Nine Course," were opened along with the hotel and are a true piece of Caribbean golf history. In fact, for a long time, this course was the only one in Barbados and one of the few in the whole of Central America.

Sandy Lane

286-287 You can admire the sea on the horizon from the beautiful holes at Sandy Lane. In Barbados golf has been popular for some time, after all, it was a British colony from 1627 to 1966. There are five golf clubs on the island today.

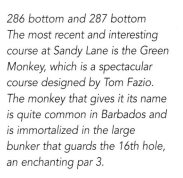

*286 bottom and 287 bottom
The most recent and interesting
course at Sandy Lane is the Green
Monkey, which is a spectacular
course designed by Tom Fazio.
The monkey that gives it its name
is quite common in Barbados and
is immortalized in the large
bunker that guards the 16th hole,
an enchanting par 3.*

*287 top The three courses at
Sandy Lane (two 18- and one
nine-hole, the famous "Old
Course," inaugurated in 1961)
are set within colorful, tropical
scenery, with palms, mahogany
trees, and large flowery bushes.*

Today, it is accompanied by two prestigious courses created by Tom Fazio, who has more courses on *Golf Digest*'s list of America's 100 Greatest Golf Courses than any other designer. Until 2005, outside of the United States and the Bahamas, Barbados was the only place in the world that could boast a course designed by this famous American architect, who never went overseas to conduct his business.

Fazio's first course at Sandy Lane was the Country Club, which was then followed by the beautiful Green Monkey. The latter is the resort's jewel and owes its names to the monkey that represents one of the island's symbols. As a homage to these cute companions, which can often be spotted on the resort's trees, Fazio had the shape of a monkey sculpted into the large bunker in front of the green on the 16th, a spectacular

par 3 played on distances of 142 to 218 yards (130 to 200 m). A very challenging par 72 from the back tees (there are a total of five starting tees for each hole), the Green Monkey is almost approachable if you choose the easier ones. The total lengths go from 5368 to 6780 yards (4900 to 6200 m), including the more advanced ladies' tees to the harder men's amateur tees. Remarkable changes in level, undulating fairways and greens, protected by huge bunkers, are the main hazards on the course.

The hardest holes we must mention are the 10th, a par 4 of about 470 yards (430 m), which is almost impossible to close on par for a medium-level player. The 18th hole has the same length and is a wide closing hole, with a green that seems to float from afar.

288-289 The Gávea Golf & Country Club, in the district of São Conrado, is one of the only two courses in Rio de Janeiro and is the oldest. It was also the first to organize the amateur championship in 1929 and the Brazil Open in 1945.

288 bottom Wooden beams and cheerful colors liven up the hall, with its wide windows facing the course.

289 Even though it is very spacious, the clubhouse (a former colonial farmhouse) is camouflaged by the thick vegetation.

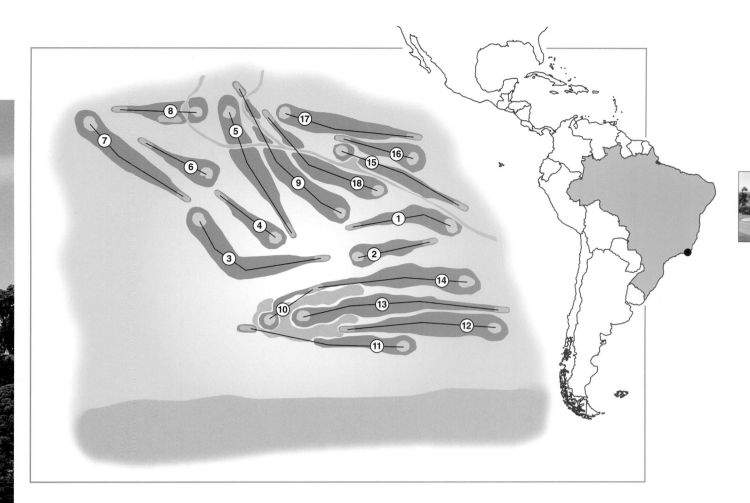

Gávea

BRAZIL

HOLE	1	2	3	4	5	6	7	8	9
YARDS	312	204	480	178	390	167	369	186	493
PAR	4	3	5	3	4	3	4	3	5

HOLE	10	11	12	13	14	15	16	17	18		TOT
YARDS	145	329	359	468	432	385	226	376	400		5899
PAR	3	4	4	5	4	4	3	4	4		69

Brazilian golf has not yet produced stars to equal those of Brazilian soccer, such as Pelé or Ronaldo. The fact is that golf has never really caught the imagination of the Brazilians, and Rio de Janeiro only offers two quality courses, which are private and reserved for members and their guests, or for guests of a few selected hotels. The two courses are the Itanhangá Golf Club and the Gávea Golf & Country Club, in the district of São Conrado. The creation of the Gávea dates back to 1920 and a group of British managers of the Companhia Tramway, Light & Power, who began to develop plans for building a golf course. Founded in 1921 as the Rio de Janeiro Golf Club, it initially opened with nine holes in 1926 but just three years later it had 18 holes (designed by the 20-year old Scotsman Arthur Morgan Davidson). The Gávea is the oldest course in Rio and has played a significant role in the history of Brazilian golf, hosting the first amateur championship in 1929 and the Brazillian Open in 1945. In the late 1920s, the club began organizing social events and was visited by the Prince of Wales, Edward, and his brother George, the Duke of Kent, who expressed their enthusiasm for the course. The president of the Argentine Republic, General Justo, also visited and he played here in 1933.

Over the years, the course underwent many alterations, some of which were made to increase the length of the holes, others were due to boundary changes. The result is that the present-day course differs quite extensively from the original one. As early as 1934, Stanley Johnson, hired to su-

pervise the works at Itanhangá, was called in to improve Gávea as well. He thought that if the land adjacent to the 11th hole could be bought, then the course could be modified so as to eliminate the holes on the mountain. He therefore presented two projects, one including the land, one without. The latter plan was chosen because purchasing the land proved impossible. So today the front nine continue to provide a rollercoaster route through the thick forest, which requires accurate shots and a good game strategy.

Nonetheless, Johnson managed to increase the length by 350 yards (320 m) by removing a pair of tennis courts to modify the tee on the 1st hole and moving back the tee on the 5th, which caused several discussions because it interfered with the polo. In the following years, more modifications to the holes were made and in 1969 a design was drawn up that would require future purchases of land.

290 top The design by Scottish architect Arthur Morgan Davidson, who was 20 years old at the time, has been modified several times over the years.

290 bottom This fairly short course, par 69 of 5899 yards (5394 m) does not require players to use their drivers too often. In any case, the thick vegetation requires accurate shots and a good game strategy.

290-291 The holes from the 10th to the 14th are very scenic and they follow the beach of São Conrado. In the background are the skyscrapers of Rio de Janeiro.

291 bottom left The opening holes follow a rollercoaster route on the mountain through the dense Tijuca forest.

291 bottom right The club was founded in 1921 as the Rio de Janeiro Golf Club. The land needed to build the course was found only a few years later, which is why the first nine holes were not opened until 1926, followed three years later by the second nine.

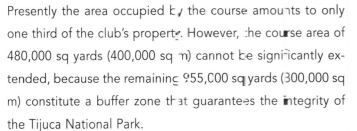

Presently the area occupied by the course amounts to only one third of the club's property. However, the course area of 480,000 sq yards (400,000 sq m) cannot be significantly extended, because the remaining 955,000 sq yards (300,000 sq m) constitute a buffer zone that guarantees the integrity of the Tijuca National Park.

The layout of the course, which is not very long, requires a lot of skill and players must use irons rather than the driver and face several hazards, including the lush surrounding vegetation.

The inbound nine holes are played partly along São Conrado beach (the 10th to the 14th) before crossing the main road and returning to the mountain and the Tijuca forest. The fairways are excellently maintained, while the greens are rather challenging and often force players to putt more than three times.

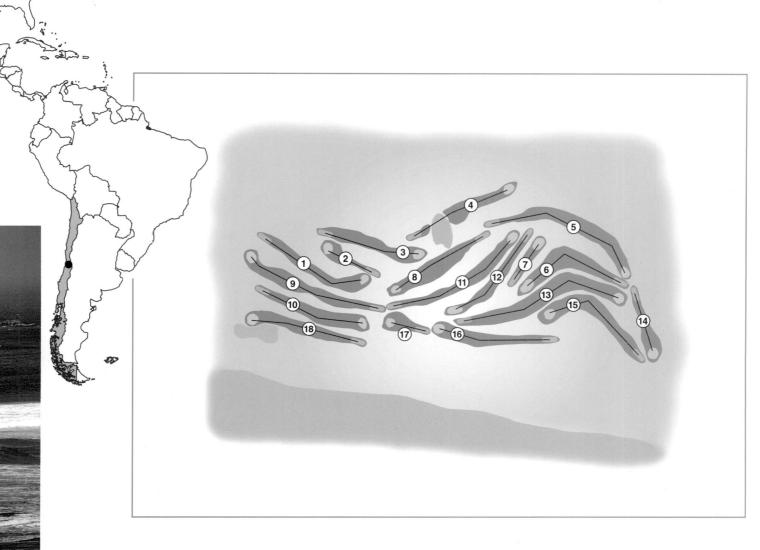

Cachagua

CHILE

HOLE	1	2	3	4	5	6	7	8	9
YARDS	370	189	388	372	514	389	150	362	479
PAR	4	3	4	4	5	4	3	4	5

HOLE	10	11	12	13	14	15	16	17	18		TOT
YARDS	370	460	336	539	157	358	387	127	418		6365
PAR	4	5	4	5	3	4	4	3	4		72

Chile has perhaps the most recognizable shape of any country in the world. Long and thin, it is 2860 miles (4600 km) from north to south but only 267 miles (430 km) across at its widest point. This means that it has a great variety of climatic and environmental conditions, from the desert in the north to the glaciers of the extreme south. More or less one third of the way in from the scorching pampas and 40 mph (60 km/h) screaming winds of Cape Horn, is Chile's most temperate belt, which experts describe as "Mediterranean." In the middle of this narrow strip of land stuck between the Pacific Ocean and the Andes is Santiago, the country's capital, while on the coast we have the port of Valparaiso and the tourist area of Viña del Mar, the most famous in Chile, with its beautiful beaches and large hotels and casinos. Going north, the coast gets wilder and less populated, despite the fact that the endless beaches seem purposely made for vacationing. About 45 minutes from Valparaiso is Cachagua, an inhabited area that faces the island of the same name, which lies just off the coast and as a nature reserve is protected against any human intrusion. It was in this area between the 1940s and 1950s that golf arrived, though it was barely popular in South America in those days. One of the area's VIPs, Nemesio Vicuña, donated some land to the future Admiral Edgardo von Schroeders, which allowed a group of friends to found the Club de Golf Cachagua. However, it was two years later, in 1954, before golfers saw the first two holes. Year after year, the course expanded until it reached nine holes. Other important years in the history of the club are the year 1987, when all

292-293 North of Valparaiso, on the northern coast of Chile, the area of Cachagua offers spectacular views. The golf club is located in an ideal area beside the Pacific Ocean, which skirts three holes of the course, among them the beautiful par-3 10th hole.

292 bottom and 293 The clubhouse and the buildings of the Golf Club Cachagua are simple and basic, but the club offers exactly what a purist golfer wants: an interesting course from a technical point of view, set in a truly unique landscape.

Cachagua

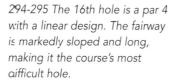

294-295 The 16th hole is a par 4 with a linear design. The fairway is markedly sloped and long, making it the course's most difficult hole.

294 bottom and 295 middle and bottom The position of the Cachagua course affords it panoramic views. A third of the holes are on higher ground to the rest of the course, and from these higher places players have spectacular views of the ocean, the beach, and the surrounding mountains.

295 top The first two holes at Cachagua were created in 1954, then others were progressively added. The most important modification happened in 2003, when the course was completely redesigned and is now 6365 yards (5820 m) long.

the native grass was replaced with Bermuda grass, which is better for golf in those weather conditions, and 1991, when some neighboring land was purchased. The Cachagua course was finally redesigned in 2003 by adding the second set of nine holes, which brought it to its present-day 6365 yards (5820 m).

Spread out next to a gorgeous sandy beach, the course is the ideal viewing point for the island of Cachagua, with its sea lions, pelicans, and many other types of birds. The accommodation facilities, which include a clubhouse with dressing rooms and a pro shop, are not that remarkable, but the course offers what true golfers seek – a technically interesting course in a truly unusual landscape.

Its position is stunning, with holes following the coastline on a slightly rolling terrain. A third of the holes are higher than the rest of the course and from these higher fairways you can admire the marvelous ocean views, the beaches, and the surrounding mountains. From a technical point of view, even if it is not that long, the Cachagua course is quite challenging thanks to an often lively wind, as well as cypress and pine patches, large rough areas, water hazards, and bunkers The 16th hole in particular must be mentioned.

It is a nice par 4 and one of the most difficult holes thanks to its narrow fairway which slopes back quite considerably. From the tee we descend along the tree-lined hollow, only to come back up towards the green, which is well protected by bunkers and vegetation. The 17th hole is the most intriguing and unfolds near the beach, where you will be pleasantly distracted by the views. If you are easily distracted, then the last hole will be a challenge as it is probably the most beautiful.

296-297 There are three nine-hole canchas (courses) at the Olivos Golf Club in Buenos Aires: the White, the Red, and the Blue. The first two are used to make the famous championship course, which has hosted ten Argentine Opens (Abierto de Argentina), the most important tournament in South America.

296 bottom and 297 The Olivos Golf Club, officially founded on 13th August 1926, was designed by Luther Koontz, an irrigation and drainage expert who also collaborated with the famous architect Alister Mackenzie in creating another beautiful Buenos Aires club, the Jockey Club.

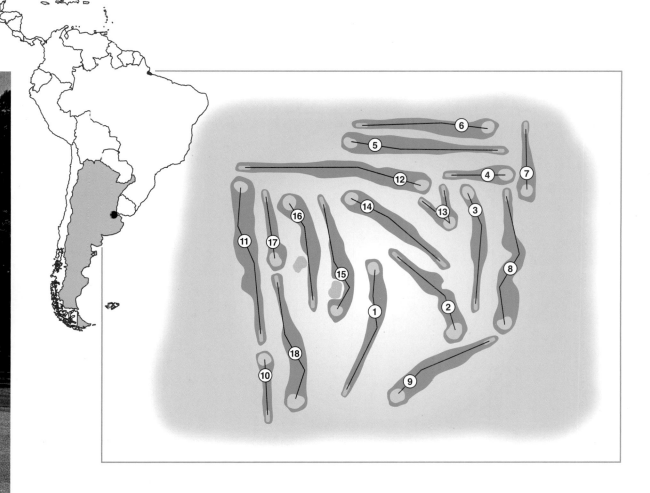

Olivos

ARGENTINA

HOLE	1	2	3	4	5	6	7	8	9
YARDS	508	385	420	178	415	415	176	502	346
PAR	5	4	4	3	4	4	3	5	4

HOLE	10	11	12	13	14	15	16	17	18		TOT
YARDS	199	557	399	162	428	470	403	210	503		6706
PAR	3	5	4	3	4	5	4	3	5		72

Many experts consider this course to be the best in South America, including *Golf Digest* which put it in the top 100 courses in the world. It also has 80 years of history, making it one of the oldest clubs in Argentina and South America. Officially inaugurated on 13th August 1926, the Olivos Golf Club is located about half an hour from downtown Buenos Aires, the capital of the republic. The 27 holes of the Olivos Golf Club stretch out along the Pan-American Highway, the famous road system that links all the mainland nations of the Americas. In South America the route starts in Buenos Aires heads west across Argentina to Chile, turns north through Chile, Peru, Ecuador, Colombia, and finally reaches Panama, where it ends with the southern arm of the "Ruta 1."

As with the other historic courses in Argentina, the Olivos Golf Club was established by a group of British citizens. The game arrived in this South American republic in 1879 when the Scotsman Henry Smith arrived in Buenos Aires carrying his golf bag. At customs this strange baggage immediately sparked the curiosity of the customs officials, and Smith, who only spoke a few words of Spanish, took a long time to convince them that his iron-headed clubs were not weapons. The Olivos Golf Club was created by English workers who, after the First World War, moved to Argentina to work on the construction of several railways. The design of the course was entrusted to Luther Koontz, an irrigation and draining expert, who helped the great Alistair Mackenzie create two other famous Buenos Aires courses within the Jockey Club, another historic club.

Originally, the Olivos was envisaged as a 36-hole course, but 27 were constructed, wider and more majestic, comprising three courses (*canchas*) distinguished by colors: Blanca (White), Colorada (Red), and Azul (blue) – respectively 3378, 3328, and 3036 yards (3089, 3044, and 2777 m) long. The Blanca and the Colorada are used to make the championship course, which is definitely the most prestigious in South America and has hosted international competitions, such as the World Amateur, the Copa del Los Andes, and ten Argentine Opens (Abierto de Argentina). The result of Koontz's work and of the subsequent refurbishing is a high-class course, definitely adhering to classic golf design principles.

298-299 and 298 bottom Next
to the Olivos Golf Club is a
unique building, the Estancia, a
veritable "castle" immersed in
the marvelous garden, where
golfers using this Buenos Aires
club can stay.

*299 The interiors of the Estancia
are beautifully decorated with
antique furniture. Thanks in part
to this magnificent building, the*

*Olivos is ranked among the best
Argentinian clubs, along with the
Jockey Club and the Buenos Aires,
all located around the capital.*

The init al idea was to create holes that were not challenging with respect to length, but rather for the choice of club, technique, and the precision of the shot. Over the years, the fundamental elements of the design remained and were enhanced by the course's maturation and the growth of beautiful trees. A true blessing, because its short length could have penalized Olivos with the competition from newer, longer courses.

On the Cancha Blanca, the 2nd and 3rd holes are rather compex, even though the hardest one is always the 5th, which requires a well-placed drive followed by a precise approach through the narrow entry to the green. The Colorada's 3rd, 4th, and 5th holes are impressive, but the biggest praise must go to the 6th, which is the 15th on the championship course. Normally, it is played by members as a par 5, but on special occasions it loses a shot and turns into one of the longest and most difficult par 4s ever, with its 470 yard (430 m) length. Ranked by *Golf Magazine* among the top 100 most beautiful holes in the world, the 15th of the Olivos is a right dogleg that today, due to the height of the trees, cannot be "cut" anymore. Defending the green, is an oval water hazard that penalizes less than precise attempts on the tough second shot to the flag. The rest of the work is done by the bunker surrounding the green, which is rather wide and slightly rolling.

ACKNOWLEDGEMENTS

The Publisher would like to thank (Golf Clubs in order of appearance in the book):

Mats Malmberg (Halmstad Golfklubb), John Duncan (Royal Dornoch Golf Club), Colin McLeod and Alison Stevenson (Carnoustie Golf Links), Mike Woodcock (St. Andrews Links Trust), David Scott (Director, Kingsbarns Golf Links), Jillian Barclay (Loch Lomond Golf Club), Charlotte Dickson and Kate Dunnion (The Westin Turnberry Resort Golf Courses), Mike Gilyeat (The Royal Birkdale Golf Club), Peter Fawcus (Royal St. Georges Golf Club), Mike Perry (Royal Porthcawl Golf Club), Seán Clancy (Portmarnock Golf Club) Simon Duffield (Ballybunion Golf Club). Hamburger Golf-Club Falkenstein, Susanne Freymann and Jens Läsker (Sporting Club Berlin Scharmützelsee), Le Golf National, Les Bordes, Gaston F. Barras President, Golf Club Crans-sur-Sierre) and Christian Barras (Golf Club Crans-sur-Sierre), Giovanni Borri (Golf Club Biella "Le Betulle"), Stefano Malinverni (President, Golf Club Castelconturbia), Nuno Bastos (Director, Aphrodite Hills Golf), Royal Golf Dar Es Salam, Alice Evans (Pezula Golf Club), Mr. Song Young Hwan (New Seoul Country Club), Delhi Golf Club, Nirwana Bali Golf Club, Banff Springs Golf Club, Alcino Affonseca (President, Gávea Golf & Country Club), Lodewijk Klootwijk (Director of EGCOA), Marcelo and Cristiana Stallone, Marcos Bellizia, Alberto Echellino, Paolo Saviolo.

The Author would like to thank:

Niall Flanagan and Neil Gray (Loch Lomond), Christos Tsiakas (Cyprus National Tourist Board), Jazia Santissi (Moroccan National Tourist Board), Barbara Gajotto (Constance Hotels), Elisa Aristo (Absolute Golf).

USEFUL ADDRESSES AND NUMBERS

Halmstad Golfklubb
Golfbanevägen
30273 Halmstad, Sweden
Tel. +46 (0)35 176800
info@halmstadgk.golf.se
www.hgk.se

Royal Dornoch Golf Club
Golf Road
Dornoch IV25 3LW
Sutherland, Scotland
Tel. –44 (0)1862 810219
rdgc@royaldornoch.com
www.royaldornoch.com

Carnoustie Golf Links
20 Links Parade
Carnoustie
Angus, Scotland
Tel. +44 (0)1241 853789
golf@carnoustiegolflinks.co.uk
www.carnoustiegolflinks.co.uk

St. Andrews Links Trust
Pilmour House, St Andrews
Fife KY15 9SF – Scotland
Tel: +44 (0) 1334 466666
Fax: +44 (0) 1334 479555
www.standrews.org.uk

Kingsbarns Golf Links
Fife KY16 8QD
Kingsbarns, Scotland
Tel. +44 (0)1334 460860
info@kingsbarns.com
www.kingsbarns.com

Loch Lomond Golf Club
Rosschu House
Luss by Alexandria
Dunbartonshire G83 8NT, Scotland
Tel. +44 (0)1436 655555
info@lochlomond.com
www.lochlomond.com

Muirfield Golf Club (Honorable Company of Edinburgh Golfers)
Muirfield
Gullane
East Lothian, Scotland
Tel. +44 (0)1620 842123
hceg@muirfield.org.uk
www.muirfield.org.uk

Royal Troon Golf Club
Craigend Road
Troon, Ayrshire, Scotland
tel. +44 (0)1292 311555
www.royaltroon.co.uk

The Westin Turnberry Resort Golf Courses
Turnberry
Ayrshire, Scotland
Tel. +44 (0)1655 331000
turnberry@westin.com
www.turnberry.co.uk

The Royal Birkdale Golf Club
Waterloo Road, Southport
Merseyside, England
Tel. +44 (0)1704 567920
secretary@royalbirkdale.com
www.royalbirkdale.com

Royal St Georges Golf Club
CT13 9PB Sandwich
Kent, England
Tel: +44 (0)1304 613090
general@royalstgeorges.com
www.royalstgeorges.com

Royal Porthcawl Golf Club
CF36 3UW Rest Bay, Porthcawl
Mid-Glamorgan, South Wales, England
Tel. +44 (0)1656 782251
www.royalporthcawl.com

Portmarnock Golf Club
Portmarnock, Co. Dublin, Ireland
Tel. +353 (0) 18462968
Fax +353 (0) 18462634
www.portmarnockgolfclub.ie

Ballybunion Golf Club
Sandhill Road
Ballybunion
County Kerry, Ireland
Tel. +353 6827146
www.ballybuniongolfclub.ie

Hamburger Golf-Club Falkenstein
In de Bargen 59
22587 Hamburg Germany
Tel. +49 40 812377
mail@hamburger-golf-club.de
www.hamburger-golf-club.de

Sporting Club Berlin Scharmützelsee
Parkalle 3
5526 Bad Saarow, Germany
Tel. +49 (0)3363 63300
golf.bsa@a-rosa.de
www.sporting-club-berlin.de

Le Golf National
Avenue du Golf
78280 Guyancourt, France
Tel. +33 (0) 130433600
www.golf-national.com

Les Bordes
41220 Saint-Laurent-Nouan, France
Tel. +33 (0) 254877213
reception@lesbordes.org
www.lesbordes.com

Valderrama Golf Club
Avda. de los Cortijos
11310 Sotogrande, Cadiz, Spain
tel. +34 956 791200
www.valderrama.com

Vilamoura Golf Club
P-8125-507 Vilamoura, Portugal
Tel. +351 289 310341
www.oceanicogolf.com

Golf Club Crans-sur-Sierre
CH 3963 Crans-sur-Sierre, Switzerland
Tel. +41 (0)27 4859797
info@golfcrans.ch
www.golfcrans.ch

Golf Club Biella "Le Betulle"
Regione Valcarozza 2
13887 Magnano Biellese (Bi), Italy
Tel. +39 (0)15 679151
info@golfclubbiella.it
www.golfclubbiella.it

Golf Club Castelconturbia
Via Castelconturbia 10
Località Bindellina
Agrate Conturbia (No), Italy
tel. +39 (0)322 832093
www.golfclubcastelconturbia.it
info@hote golfconturbia.com

Le Méridien Moscow Country Club
Nakhabino, Krasnogorsky District
143 430 Russian Federation
Tel. +7 (0)95 9263911
www.mccmembers.ru

Aphrodite Hills Golf
Aphrodite Avenue 2
8509 Kouklia, Cyprus
Tel. +357 26828200
www.aphroditehills.com

Royal Golf Dar Es Salam
Avenue Imam Malik, km 9
Souissi, Rabat, Morocco
Tel. +212 (0) 37755864/5
golfdaressalam@menara.ma
www.royalgolfdaressalam.com

Pezula Golf Club
Lagoonview Drive, Western Cape

Knysna, South Africa
Tel. +27 (0)44 3025307
info@pezula.com
www.pezula.com

Constance Belle Mare Plage
Poste de Flacq, Mauritius
Tel. +230 402 2600
golfpro@bellemareplagehotel.com
www.bellemareplagehotel.com

Emirates Golf Club
Sheikh Zayed Rd.
P.O. Box 24040
Dubai, United Arab Emirates
Tel. +971 4 3801234
www.dubaigolf.com

Spring City Golf & Lake Resort
TangChi, YiLiang - Kunming
Yunnan, China 652103
Tel. + 86 871 7671188 Ext.1122
frontoffice@springcityresort.com
www.springcityresort.com

Mission Hills Golf Club
Shenzen, China
Tel. +86 755 2802 0888
info@missionhillsgroup.com
www.missionhillsgroup.com

New Seoul Country Club
Samdong, Gwangju-si,
Gyounggi-do 464-040, Seoul, Korea
Tel. +31 762 5672

Delhi Golf Club
Dr. Zakir Hussain Road
New Delhi, India
Tel. +91 11 2436 5105
delhigolfclub@vsnl.net
www.delhigolfclub.org

Blue Canyon Country Club
165, Moo1, Thepkasattri Road, Thalang
Phuket, Thailand
Tel. +66 76 328088
www.bluecanyonclub.com

Hirono Golf Club
Miki-shi
Hyogo, Japan
Tel. +81 794 85 0123

Nirwana Bali Golf Club
Jl. Raya Tanah Lot
Kediri, Tanaban
82171 Bali, Indonesia
Tel. +62 361 815960

reservation@nirwanabaligolf.com
www.nirwanabaligolf.com

New South Wales Golf Club
Henry Head
Botany Bay National Park - La Perouse
New South Wales 2036, Australia
Tel. +61 2 96614455
admin@nswgolfclub.com.au
www.nswgolfclub.com.au

The Royal Melbourne Golf Club
Cheltenham Road
Black Rock, Victoria, Australia
Tel. +613 95986755
www.royalmelbourne.com

Cape Kidnappers Golf Course
448 Clifton Road
Te Awanga, Hawke's Bay
North Island, New Zealand
Tel. +64 6 8751900
www.capekidnappers.com

Banff Springs Golf Club
405 Spray Avenue
T1L1J4 Banff, Alberta (Canada)
Tel. +1 403 7622211
www.banffspringsgolfclub.com

Pebble Beach Golf Links
The Lodge at Pebble Beach
1700 17 Mile Drive
Pebble Beach, California 93953 (USA)
Tel. +1 831 6243811
www.pebblebeach.com

Cypress Point Golf Club
17 Mile Drive
Pebble Beach, California (USA)
Tel. +1 831 6246444

Shinnecock Hills Golf Club
200 Tuckahoe Road
Southampton, New York (USA)
Tel. +1 631 2833525

Oakmont Country Club
1233 Hulton Road
Oakmont, Pennsylvania 15139 (USA)
Tel. +1 412 8288000
www.oakmont-countryclub.org

Baltusrol Golf Club
201 Shunpike Road
Springfield, New Jersey 07081 (USA)
Tel. +1 973 3761900
clukova@baltusrol.org
www.baltusrol.org

Pinehurst Resort
1 Carolina Vista Drive
Pinehurst, North Carolina (USA)
Tel. +1 910 2358125
www.pinehurst.com

Augusta National Golf Club
2604 Washington Road
Augusta, Georgia 30904 (USA)
Tel. +1 706 6676000
www.augusta.com

Poipu Bay
2250 Ainako St., Koloa
Kauai, Hawaii (USA)
Tel. +1 808 7428711
www.poipubay.com

Mid Ocean Club
Tucker's Town
Tel. +1 441 2930330
info@themidoceanclubbermuda.com
www.themidoceanclubbermuda.com

Cabo del Sol
Los Cabos, Baja California, Mexico
Tel. +52 624 1458200/1
www.cabodelsol.com/
content/golf_ocean.html

Casa de Campo
La Romana
Dominican Republic
Tel. +1 809 5233333
www.casadecampo.com.do

Sandy Lane
St. James, Barbados
West Indies BB24024
Tel. +1 246 4442000
www.sandylane.com

Gávea Golf & Country Club
Estrada da Gávea, 800
São Conrado, Rio de Janeiro
Tel. +55 21 33236050
www.gaveagolf.com.br

Club de Golf Cachagua
Cachagua, Chile
Tel. +56 33771001
www.clubdegolfcachagua.cl

Olivos Golf Club
Ruta Panamericana Ramal Pilar Km 32
Ing. Pablo.Nogués CP 1613
Buenos Aires, Argentina
Tel. +54 114587
www.olivosgolf.com.ar

PHOTO CREDITS

Eduardo Abad/epa/Corbis: pages 106-107
David Alexander/Getty Images: pages 40, 41 top, 41 center, 41 bottom, 158 right, 186, 186-187, 187 bottom, 190-191, 192-193, 194 bottom, 194-195, 195 left, 195 right, 196 top, 196 center, 196-197, 197, 238 bottom, 238-239, 240 top and center, 240-241, 241 left and right, 243 top, center and bottom, 245, 246-247, 247 top, center and bottom, 248-249, 249 top, center and bottom
Courtesy of the Aphrodite Hill Golf Course: pages 134, 135 bottom, 136 left, 136 bottom, 136-137, 137 top, 137 center, 137 bottom, 138 top, 138 center, 138 bottom
Courtesy of the A-ROSA Resorts: pages 92 bottom, 92-93, 93, 94, 95 top
Atlantide Phototravel/Corbis: page 285 bottom
Courtesy of the Banff Springs Golf Club: pages 222 center, 224-225, 226, 226-227, 227 top, 227 center, 227 bottom
Franco Barbagallo: pages 296, 296-297, 297 bottom, 298, 298-299, 299 top and bottom
Graham Bell/Alamy: page 79 right
Marcello Bertinetti/Archivio White Star: pages 114-115, 115 bottom, 116 bottom
Carlo Borlenghi/SEASEE.COM: pages 122-123, 125 left
Simon Bruty/Getty Images: pages 232-233
Courtesy of the Cachagua Golf Club: pages 274 center, 292, 292-293, 293 center, 294, 294-295, 295 top, 295 center, 295 bottom
Matt Campbell/epa/Corbis: pages 250, 254 bottom
David Cannon/Getty Images: pages 16 right, 19 center right, 20-21, 21, 22 center, 22-23, 24 bottom, 27 top, 29, 31, 32, 33 bottom, 54-55, 55 top, 55 bottom, 57, 58 left, 58 right, 64 right, 65 center, 75 top, 75 bottom, 76-77, 82-83, 84 right, 86, 94-95, 95 bottom, 100-101, 102-103, 151 bottom, 163 top, 164 center, 164-165, 165, 166 left, 167, 168-169, 180, 182 top, 183, 192 bottom, 205 bottom, 214 center, 217, 219 center and bottom, 220 top and center top, 220-221, 223, 228 top, 228 bottom, 228-229, 229, 237
Matt Cardy/Getty Images: page 76
Mathew Cavanaugh/epa/Corbis: page 236 top
Angelo Colombo/Archivio White Star: pages 6-7, 19 top, 19 center left, 24 top, 28 top, 36 top, 36-37, 43 top 46, 53 top, 56 top, 56-57, 60 top, 69 top, 72 top, 77 top, 80 top, 85 top, 88 top, 92 top, 96 top, 100 top, 105 top, 110, 115 top, 122 top, 127, 130 top, 135 top, 142 top, 147 top, 151 top, 161 top, 164 top, 171 top, 174 top, 181 top, 187 top, 194 top, 198 top, 205 top, 210 top, 214 top, 225 top, 230 top, 235 top, 238 top, 244 top, 251 top, 256 top, 260 top, 264-265, 270 top, 276, 281 top, 285 top, 289 top, 293 top, 297 top
Diane Cook & Len Jenshel: page 259 left and right
Diane Cook & Len Jenshel/Corbis: pages 258-259, 282 top right
Danita Delimont/Alamy: pages 270-271
T. & H. Deprez: pages 116-117, 117, 119 top, 119 center bottom, 120-121
Mike Ehrmann/Getty Images: pages 254-255
Don Feria/Corbis: pages 264-265
Jonathan Ferrey/Getty Images: pages 20, 22 top, 258
Donald Ford: pages 4-5, 16 left, 32-33, 33 top, 30 bottom, 30-31, 38-39, 39 top, 39 bottom, 44 center, 44-45, 54-55
Robert Fried/Alamy: pages 278-279
Stuart Franklin/Getty Images: pages 46-47, 47, 56 bottom, 158 left, 159, 170, 172 top, 173, 180-181, 181 center, 182 bottom, 184-185, 185 top, 185 bottom, 242-243

Courtesy of the Gavea: pages 275, 288, 288-289, 289 center, 290 top, 290 bottom, 290-291, 291 left, 291 right
Getty Images: pages 253 bottom, 286-287
Courtesy of the Golf Club Biella "Le Betulle": pages 122 bottom, 123, 124 top, 124 center, 124-125, 125 right
Courtesy of the Golf Club Castelconturbia: pages 126, 126-127, 128, 128-129, 129
Sam Greenwood/WireImage/Getty Images: page 252
Otto Greule Jr/Getty Images: page 267 left
Rough Guides/Alamy: pages 110-111
Scott Halleran/Getty Images: pages 49, 244-245, 270 bottom
Courtesy of the Halmstad Golfklubb: pages 18 left, 18 right, 18-19, 22 bottom
Courtesy of the Hamburger Golf-Club: pages 88 bottom, 88-89, 89, 90 top, 90 bottom, 90-91, 91
Richard Heathcote/Getty Images: pages 53 bottom, 79 left, 111, 113 top, 170-171, 172 bottom, 172-173
Eric Hepwort: pages 61, 69 bottom
Tommy Hindley/Professional Spo/NewSport/Corbis: page 35 bottom
John Hios: pages 134-135, 139
Robert Holmes/Alamy: pages 40-41
Harry How/Getty Images: pages 52-53, 236 center, 254 center
Phil Inglis/Getty Images: pages 60 bottom, 67 bottom
The Irish Image Collection/Corbis: page 87
Courtesy of the Kingsbarns Golf Links: pages 42, 42-43, 43 bottom
Ross Kinnaird/Getty Images: pages 59 top and bottom, 114, 284-285, 286, 287 bottom
Darren Kirk/Alamy: page 30 top
Peter Klaunzer/epa/Corbis: page 116 top
Courtesy of the Les Bordes Golf International: pages 100 bottom, 101, 102 center, 103 left, 103 right
Courtesy of the Legend Golf Course, Links Golf Course-Constance Belle Mare Plage-Mauritius: pages 140 right, 141, 150, 150-151, 152 top, 152 bottom, 152-153, 153, 154, 155 top, 155 bottom, 156, 156-157, 157
Courtesy of the Le Méridien Moscow Country Club: pages 130 bottom, 131, 133
Courtesy of the Le Meridien Nirvana Golf & Spa Resort: pages 198 center and bottom, 199, 200, 200-201
Matthew Lewis/Getty Images: pages 35 center, 44 bottom
Gary Lisbon Golf Photography: pages 2-3, 202 left and right, 203, 204, 206-207, 207 top and bottom, 208-209, 209 top and bottom, 210 center, 211, 212 top, 212 center, 213, 215, 216 top, 216 center, 216 bottom, 216-217, 218-219, 219 top, 220 center bottom, 220 bottom
Christian Liewig/Corbis: page 35 top
Patrick Lim: pages 158 center, 166 bottom, 166-167, 168, 169 top, 169 bottom, 188 top, 188 bottom, 188-189, 189, 191 top and bottom
Warren Little/Getty Images: pages 34-35, 56 center, 77 bottom, 78, 78-79, 112, 112-113, 113 bottom
Courtesy of the Loch Lomond Golf Club: pages 48 top, 48 center, 48 bottom, 48-49, 50, 50 center top, 50 center bottom, 50 bottom, 50-51, 51 left, 51 right
London Aerial Photo Library/Corbis: pages 60-61
Iain Lowe: pages 24-25, 26-27
Andy Lyons/Getty Images: page 231
John G. Mabanglo/epa/Corbis: page 262 left
Ludovic Maisant/Corbis: page 284

Hunter Martin/Getty Images: page 264 bottom
Leo Mason/Corbis: page 38
Buddy Mays/Corbis: page 225 bottom
Joe McNally/Getty Images: pages 182-183
Mediacolor's/Alamy: page 287 top
Patrick Micheletti: pages 96 bottom, 96-97, 97, 98, 98-99, 99 left, 99 right
Donald Miralle/Getty Images: pages 14-15, 234, 234-235, 235 bottom
Brian Morgan/Alamy: page 274 right
Brian Morgan/Getty Images: page 17
Brian D. Morgan: pages 25, 102 top, 105 bottom, 106 top and bottom, 119 bottom, 130-131, 132 top, 132 bottom, 132-133, 232, 233 top and bottom, 271, 272, 272-273, 273, 274 left, 276-277, 278, 279 top, 280-281, 282 bottom, 283
Paul Mounce/Corbis: page 222 right
Stephen Munday/Getty Images: pages 52, 55 center, 140 left
Courtesy of the New Seoul Country Club: pages 174 bottom, 174-175, 175, 176 top, 176 center top, 176 center bottom, 176 bottom, 176-177, 177, 178 top, 178 center, 178 bottom, 178-179, 179
Gary Newkirk/Getty Images: page 256 center
Gary Newkirk/NewSport/Corbis: page 262 bottom
Guang Niu/Getty Images: page 185 right
M. Timothy O'Keefe/Alamy: pages 280, 281 bottom
Douglas Peebles/Corbis: page 257
Courtesy of the Pezula Championship Course, Knysna, South Africa: pages 146, 146-147, 147 center, 148, 148-149, 149 top, 149 bottom
Courtesy of the Portmarnock Hotel & Golf Links: pages 80 bottom, 82, 83 top, 83 center, 83 bottom
Andrew Redington/Getty Images: pages 44 top, 68, 70 top, 70-71, 80-81, 84-85, 118-119, 119 center top, 161 center, 162-163, 163 center, 163 bottom
Tony Roberts/Corbis: pages 12-13, 54, 64 left, 68-69, 251 bottom, 252-253, 253 top, 267 right, 269 top and bottom, 277, 282 top left
Courtesy of the Royal Golf Dar Es-Salam: pages 142 center, 142 bottom, 142-143, 143, 144 left, 144 right, 144-145, 145 top, 145 bottom
Courtesy of the Royal St. Georges Golf Club: page 73
Ezra Shaw/Getty Images: pages 230-231, 239
Phil Sheldon Golf Picture Library/SEASEE.COM: pages 26, 27 bottom, 28 bottom, 28-29, 36 center, 36 bottom, 37, 67 top, 70 bottom, 71, 72 bottom, 72-73, 74, 74-75, 81, 84 left, 85 center, 86-87, 104, 104-105, 107, 108 top, 108 center, 108 bottom, 108-109, 160-161, 171 center and bottom, 210-211, 236-237, 250-251, 254 top, 260 bottom, 260-261, 261, 262-263, 266-267, 268-269
Witold Skrypczak/Alamy: pages 222 left, 244 center
Herbert Spichtinger/zefa/Corbis: page 201 top
Matthew Stockman/Getty Images: page 9
Torleif Svensson/Corbis: page 16 center
George Tiedemann/NewSport/Corbis: page 230 bottom
Greg Trott/Getty Images: pages 263, 264 top
Greg Vaughn/Alamy: page 279 bottom
Ian Walton/Getty Images: pages 192 top, 192 center
Courtesy of the Westin Turnberry Resort: pages 62, 62-63, 63 top left, 63 top right, 63 center, 65 top, 66-67
Martin Westlake/Asia Images/Getty Images: page 201 bottom
Paul White/Alamy: pages 58-59
Stefan Zaklin/epa/Corbis: page 160

INDEX

© 2008 White Star S.p.A.
Via Candido Sassone, 22/24
13100 Vercelli, Italy
www.whitestar.it

Translation Marco Visentin

All rights reserved. This book, or any portion thereof, may not
be reproduced in any form without written permission of the
publisher. WS White Star Publishers® is a registered trademark
property of White Star S.p.A.

ISBN 978-88-544-0400-7

REPRINTS:
1 2 3 4 5 6   12 11 10 09 08

Printed in China

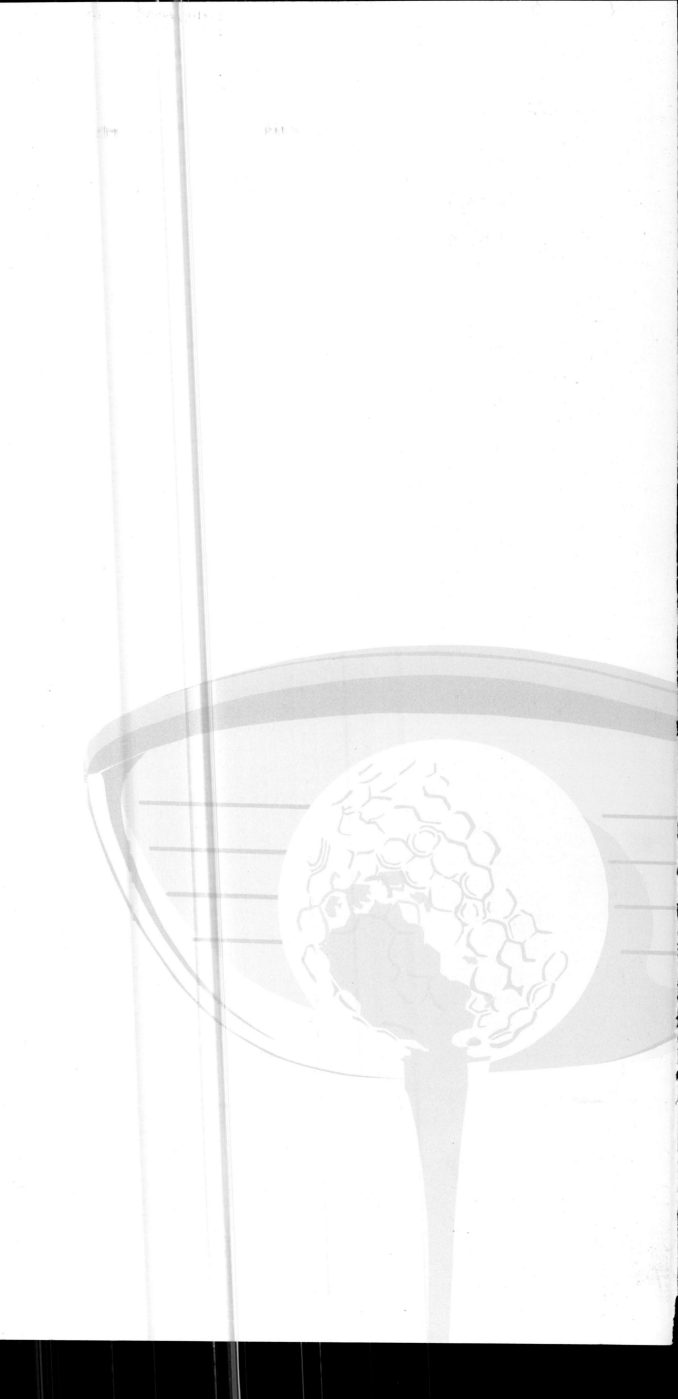

GOLF
AROUND THE WORLD

The Great Game and Its Most Spectacular Courses

WHITE STAR PUBLISHERS

MAIN LIBRARY
Champaign Public Library
200 West Green Street
Champaign Illinois 61820-5193

W9-AJX-058

THIS GIFT TO THE
CHAMPAIGN PUBLIC LIBRARY
IS PRESENTED BY

Champaign Public Library Staff

IN MEMORY OF

James B. Carter

Champaign Public Library
Foundation